MENCKEN REVISITED

MENCKEN REVISITED

Author, Editor
& Newspaperman

S.L. Harrison

with a prologue by
Russell Baker

University Press of America
Lanham • New York • Oxford

Copyright © 1999 by
S. L. Harrison

University Press of America,® Inc.
4720 Boston Way
Lanham, Maryland 20706

12 Hid's Copse Rd.
Cumnor Hill, Oxford OX2 9JJ

Library of Congress Cataloging-in-Publication Data

Harrison, S. L. (Stanley L.).
Mencken revisited : author, editor & newspaperman / S. L. Harrison
; with a prologue by Russell Baker.
p.   cm.
Includes index.
1. Mencken, H. L. (Henry Louis), 1880-1956. 2. Authors,
American—20th century Biography. 3. Journalists—United States
Biography. 4. Editors—United States Biography. I. Title.
PS3525.E43Z582 1999 818'.5209—dc21 99—28419 CIP

ISBN 0-7618-1450-7 (pbk: alk. ppr.)

$52

OCLC
41439553

⊖™ The paper used in this publication meets the minimum
requirements of American National Standard for Information
Sciences—Permanence of Paper for Printed Library Materials,
ANSI Z39.48—1984

Dedicated to

The Mencken Society

and the Society's long-time President,

Arthur J. Gutman

The Sacred Cow of Baltimore

December 7, 1989, *The Sun*. [Uncaptioned - title added.]

H.L. Mencken, the "Sage of Baltimore," unquestionably the most renowned writer to emerge from "the Queen City of the Chesapeake," was accused thirty years after his death of anti-Semitic and other nefarious literary "crimes" based on a new generation's definition of correctness. This cartoon by Kevin Kallaugher (KAL), editorial cartoonist of The Sun, *would have delighted Mencken, a thorough-going iconoclast.*

Contents

Illustrations:

Cartoons:

Acknowledgments

SOME OF THESE ESSAYS appeared in different form elsewhere and served as a basis for the revised and rewritten materials presented here. Each of these essays stands alone; consequently, some repetition is inevitable but each discussion focuses on a different aspect of the multifaceted career of Henry Louis Mencken. The original versions, titles, dates and places of publication are:

From *Menckeniana* (Enoch Pratt Free Library, Baltimore, Md.): "Meeting Mencken" (Summer 1990); "Talent Scout," appeared as "Mencken and Duffy," (Spring 1994); "Money Matters" appeared as "Fiscal Mencken: An Accounting," (Spring 1995); "Editorial Guidelines" was based on "Mencken's Advice to Editors," (Winter 1995).

From *The Journal of American Culture* (Bowling Green State University), "The Scopes Trial: Mencken's Media Circus," appeared as "The Scopes `Monkey Trial Revisited: Mencken and the Editorial Art of Edmund Duffy," (Winter 1994); "Prejudice Without Discrimination," appeared as "Mencken Redoux" (Winter 1990).

From *American Journalism* (University of Georgia), "Marching Into the Millennium" appeared as "Magnificent Anachronism: A Bibliographic Essay," (Winter 1995).

Grateful thanks is due to each of the editors–Wallace Eberhard, Charles Fecher, and Ray Browne–who ventured these observations into print and to the several institutions for permission to base these essays on the original versions: the University of Georgia, Bowling Green State University, and the Enoch Pratt Free Library. Thanks also to Russell Baker for permission to include "Death in the Family" from "The Observer," © 1999 by *The New York Times*. Reprinted by permission.

The cartoon on page *vi* is reproduced with permission of KAL (Kevin Kallaugher), courtesy *The Sun,* Baltimore; Edmund Duffy's cartoons and drawings are reproduced with the permission of Sara Anne Duffy Chermayeff. The author thanks the Times Mirror Corporation, owners of *The Sun* and assets of the now-defunct *Evening Sun,* for permission to reproduce the cartoons and editorial pages. Copyright © 1999 Times-Mirror.

Thanks to the Enoch Pratt Free Library, trustee of the Mencken estate, for permission to use H.L. Mencken quotes from several sources.

A special word of thanks is owed Charles Fecher for his encouragement and Vincent Fitzpatrick, of the Enoch Pratt, who shared a portion of his treasured Mencken papers. Similarly, Hal Williams provided guidance and has been helpful with editorial comments. John Stampone was kind enough to share his memories of Duffy and Mencken. Gail Shivel is owed special thanks for reading and assisting with preparing these pages for publication.

Annie and Kit Kat, two furry friends, provided company; Mencken preferred his pet turtles, but cats are better companions. Finally, thanks to Frances June, who indulged me to work more on Mencken matters and less on mowing fields than was entirely proper.

Any errors of fact or interpretation are the fault of the author.

Introduction

THIS COLLECTION HAS a two-fold purpose: to provide an introduction to Henry Louis Mencken and to encourage a wider acquaintance for modern readers.

These essays highlight portions of Mencken's fascinating career focusing on specific areas to provide further illumination for readers familiar with HLM. Beyond that, they may stimulate readers unfamiliar with Mencken to seek his writing in print and hunt out the books that can be found in any good library.

H. L. Mencken (1880-1956) was a prodigious writer–author of more than three dozen books, editor of two magazines of national significance, literary critic, social commentator, and a noted newspaperman throughout his professional career. His writings retain the capacity to arouse readers to anger and outrage or prompt roars of approval and hearty laughter.

More people today talk about Mencken than actually sit down and read him–or sit down and read anything for that matter. But Mencken can be considered a serious historian along with his other accomplishments. Much of what he wrote–the people, the politics, and events–were the compelling issues of his time. His perceptive observations yield genuine historical analyses. However biased these may have been (and Mencken was biased), he captured the personalities and events of his times as if these had been preserved in Baltic amber, if prose of such clarity and sparkle can be compared to amber.

Go to the source and see what Mencken himself wrote about so many things. Many readers are certain to disagree with what Mencken said, but all who make that exploration will be enlightened and entertained.

A number of excellent biographies of Mencken exist (with more to come, certainly), but this is no biography. These

accounts provide only a brief introduction to HLM and his tumultuous career. A number of Mencken works and works about
Mencken are mentioned; the listing is by no means inclusive nor
are the contents intended to cite every relevant work.
Consequently, a number of books are omitted that perhaps
should be included; the author assumes full responsiblity for
these slights. My purpose is modest: to introduce Mencken and
guide the reader into interesting and hitherto unexplored paths.

Prologue

Death in the Family

Russell Baker

BALTIMORE WAS A LITERATE BLUE-COLLAR town when *The Evening Sun* was in its glory, and now there are no blue-collar towns left, illiterate has become the national style and *The Evening Sun* is finished. "Kaput," as F. Millard Foard liked to say when forecasting the future of some wretched dilatory student in his high school German class. "Kaput" with last Friday's final edition.

Baltimore was the kind of town whose public high schools offered German in 1939, and many students took it. There was a strain of sober, old-fashioned German culture from long-ago immigrations, and there was an incoming tide of new German culture being brought by Jewish refugees from Hitler.

More importantly, German was still the language in which a lot of scientific research papers were published, and the public high schools were filled with students aiming for careers in science and medicine. High school was not too early to get a jump on the future. High school was where you practiced to be an adult.

I don't want to overdo the violin music here, because Baltimore well into the 1960's was also a mean, segregated race town which did not spend a lot of its resources to brighten the future for black children. White Baltimore and black Baltimore were alien planets, almost entirely ignorant of each other.

White Baltimore, at least, was content to leave it that way. In this, it was encouraged by *The Evening Sun,* by William

The Evening Sun, April 20, 1938

Randolph Hearst's *News-Post* (long since gone to glory) and by the *Sunpapers'* morning paper, *The Sun,* which still survives under the ownership of the Los Angeles-based Times Mirror Company.

All made a point of identifying as "Negro" any person of African bloodline who chanced into their columns. Few did so, except in crime stories, and even crime stories had to be faintly amusing or uniquely dreadful or involve a white person to qualify for publication.

The doom of *The Evening Sun* was no surprise. This is a bad age for afternoon newspapers. Television, which gets blamed for everything from dandruff to George Steinbrenner, takes the rap again here.

No American of the modern strain will sit in the parlor of an evening struggling in the coils of journalistic prose when he can lean back and treat his eyeballs to the 1,001 Nights available to channel surfers. So goes the explanation, but it omits the equally fatal role of the automobile.

Blue-collar Baltimore of *The Evening Sun's* glory days rode the streetcar. Ten cents each way carried it all the way to Bethlehem Steel's big plant at Sparrows Point. Two cents bought an evening paper.

Those streetcars were full of readers, who in their modern manifestation, have become motorists inching their way through nerve-frazzling traffic while nerve-frazzling radio voices fill their wheeled boxes with a constant stream of alarms.

It's unfair that television should be so tirelessly abused while the evil automobile gets away scot free. Scholars interested in the decline of literacy ought to look at the destruction

---

Opposite: A front page from the Evening Sun *during H. L. Mencken's tenure as editorial page editor. Only one by-line; and excepting the Washington story on relief, every item is from an Associated Press dispatch. Sixty years ago, the paper had few news bureaus. Today's papers run far fewer page-one stories.*

of American mass transit systems by the Eisenhower Administration, General Motors and the auto lobby in the 1950's.

A nation sentenced to spend its networking life behind steering wheels is unlikely to read anything but traffic signs.

Whatever dooms afternoon newspapers, mourning their death is as silly as mourning the death of the Super Chief to Los Angeles or the Michelangelo to Naples. Change happens, as the bumper stickers crow. Good things lose it and die. Way of the world and so forth.

Before shuffling dry-eyed out of the chapel, however, we ought to note that *The Evening Sun* was H. L. Mencken's paper. What a monument Mencken was to American journalism. What a sad comment on the state of journalism today that it has produced no one in his league when it comes to exposing the frauds, quacks, clowns, mountebanks and imbeciles–sorry, Henry, for stealing your lexicon–who dominate American life today.

I cannot guess what the young Mencken would have said of his paper's end. But contemplating his own, he once wrote: "If, after I depart this vale, you ever remember me and have thought to please my ghost, forgive some sinner and wink your eye at some homely girl."

Chapter One

Meeting Mencken

IN THE 1940S ALMOST EVERY INHABITANT of Baltimore had heard of H. L. Mencken. Residents knew this native son brought renown to Baltimore, whether or not they were acquainted with any of his books or read a word of his writings. Baltimoreans were also aware that whatever Mencken's worldly fame, his base of operations was with the local *Sunpapers*. Neither adornment to the Monumental City was universally loved, however.

In our house, my father was a faithful subscriber to all three *Sunpapers*, though he preferred Hearst's daily *News-Post* for its superior racing results and the Sunday *American* for its lavish comic section. Nevertheless, dad read Mencken's *Evening Sun* column. He hated Mencken. (Mother simply avoided reading "that awful man.")

Dad routinely described Mencken as a "damned Dutchman," whose patriotism was in serious question. In times of greater stress he was denounced as "a goddamned krauthead." These and other ethnic descriptions were common conversational coinage in Baltimore, as Russell Baker (a former *Sun* man and Baltimorean of that era) observed in the *New York Times*. Mencken was read but not welcomed. No Mencken books were housed in our shelves; Zane Grey westerns, Wilkie Collins mysteries, and Kathleen Norris and Fannie Hurst sagas held pride of place.

After reading some Mencken newspaper columns for myself, I sought out his books at the local branch of the Enoch Pratt Free

Library. Only little exploration explained my parents' concern with the ideas Mencken provoked. Mencken was rightly viewed as a trouble-maker who raised serious questions about most things sacred to middle-class morality.   True, he had been against Prohibition, but was a suspect Democrat who hated President Franklin Delano Roosevelt.   Roosevelt was revered in our household.   Further, Mencken's strong pro-German sympathies, expressed at the outbreak of World War II and earlier in 1914, were neither forgiven nor forgotten.   Mencken was un-American and his antipathy toward religion in general, and Methodists in particular, put him under a darker cloud.

Nevertheless, when I gained entry into the *Sun* as a copy boy (a term permissible before political correctness), I set out with some purpose to meet the great man himself. Mencken was neither accessible nor easily approached. But he was on the premises from time to time. Despite what some historian-academicians assert, i.e., that Mencken left the newspaper in the early 1940s and did not return until 1948, Mencken maintained an office in the *Sunpapers* building then located at Baltimore and Charles Streets (Sun Square in old Baltimore).   The rear entrance used by most employees was a block below on Redwood Street, renamed thus from German Street during the patriotic fervor and Teutonic animosity aflame during the Great War. That portion of downtown Baltimore would quake every evening when the giant underground presses rumbled into life to print the morning *Sun*'s 8:00 p.m. Bulldog edition.

Mencken's office was off the *Sun*'s newsroom. The city room itself was a sanctuary off limits to advertising people and other commercial lesser-lights; it was reserved strictly for the working press and presided over by Charles H. Dorsey. Baker describes Dorsey magnificently in *The Good Years* and recalls his problem as a young reporter in calling his mentor "Buck." No copy boy would even think to do so. For me, Mr. Dorsey remains Mr. Dorsey.

Dorsey presided over his newsroom with regal and imperious grace and the benign benevolence of an absolute dictator. He would sit frequently tilted back at a perilous angle, with feet resting nonchalantly on his desk (a posture that I do not recollect anyone else assuming even in the late hours of the lobster

shift, not when Dorsey was around). Puffing away with his ciga-
rette clamped into a long, expensive holder, of the type favored
by President Roosevelt, Dorsey was God–the Old Testament version. That is to say, an editor of the old school.

My relations with Mr. Dorsey were excellent, however. The
morning *Sun* shift for copy boys and other lowly creatures began
at 4:00 in the afternoon. Released from classes at 2:30 or there-
abouts, I hopped on a No. 17 streetcar nearby City College (a
high school) and was in the office in downtown Baltimore shortly after 3:00. Public transportation in that era was cheap, fast,
and convenient.

In those ancient days, one of the duties of a copy boy was to
first ready-up the office: clean and fill pastepots, lay out ample
supplies of copy paper with sufficient supplies of well-sharpened
Ebony-Jet pencils to last through the night, check typewriter ribbons, distribute wire copy and flimsies to the appropriate desks
and make certain that the array of teletype machines were supplied with rolls of paper. Last, check on the telegraph operators
to see if they wanted early coffee. Perhaps you might be asked to
punch out the tape for the Trans-Lux that graced the *Sunpaper's*
building with a message that spelled out the latest news. I performed these chores well before the shift began, at first giving little notice to the silent figure, Dorsey, often presiding alone over
a quiet newsroom before the hectic frenzy of putting together
that day's edition.

One afternoon Mr. Dorsey beckoned me to his desk.
Normally, he usually would bark "copy" in a voice I can hear to
this day. Dorsey asked me who I was. Copy boys were anony-
mous. We were all, some half-dozen, known collectively as
"copy," turnover was frequent and names were earned only after
diligent service.

Our duties were to run copy to the Composing Room, fetch
back proofs to the correct desk and editor, carry photos and artwork down to the Engraving Room, keep a constant and watch-
ful eye on the Associated Press and other wire service teletype
machines, and perform whatever other errands the staff directed. Requests were frequent and often conflicting. Laggards were
not tolerated and once summoned to Mr. Dorsey's desk with a
specific tone, and after a few words, off miscreants would go with

a paymaster's chit, never to be seen again.

I told Mr. Dorsey my name. No complaints, but no compliments, either. Merely a nod. He then proceeded to give me precise and specific instructions for delivering mail and materials into that portion of the office known as "brain alley," hidden away behind closed doors.

This was the arcane area where Edmund Duffy, the cartoonist, worked; realm of the owner and publisher, where lofty editorial writers labored and read magazines and out-of-town newspapers and other interesting journals. Here H. L. Mencken maintained his office. No one ventured into this domain without specific purpose. Mr. Dorsey posited me with clear, limited assignment to carry out specific, needed deliveries and tasked me to this chore daily. I was to do it and go. And bother no one.

After a few weeks, I ventured to inquire of Dorsey, "Is it possible to meet Mr. Mencken?"

"Why do you want to meet Mencken?," Dorsey asked in an even, somehow ominous tone.

"Well, I've read his books and he's a great newspaperman. I want to be a newspaperman."

"Come along."

We entered the long corridor, passed a number of closed doors and came to an open office, where a somewhat pudgy man sat silently reading his mail. His glasses were perched on his forehead. It was Mencken himself, chewing absently on an unlit cigar.

"Henry, here's someone to meet you," Mr. Dorsey said.

He glanced at me with a hint of a smile and said, "He's read all your books and thinks you're a great newspaperman." With that he left.

Mencken pulled off his glasses, leaned back and said,

"Read all my books, heh?"

At that moment I knew that I had made a major mistake.

"Well," I said, "I have read *Newspaper Days, Happy Days* and *Heathen Days*. And I'm reading *A Treatise on the Gods.*" Actually, I had attempted to read that book and was totally awash in a flood of opinionated theological argument that I cannot quite fathom to this day.

"Well, you've still got a lot more to read. What'd you think?"

Not willing to become enmeshed in religious doctrine, I did manage to say that I really liked *Newspaper Days*. Mencken asked what I had learned. I replied that I found out what the word 'halcyon' meant. I pronounced it phonetically–'halcon.' "Halcyon," he said, pronouncing the word correctly.

"So, you want to be a newspaperman, hah? Well, I suggest you go to school."

I reminded him that he himself had not. Mencken finished his formal schooling as a graduate of Baltimore's Polytechnic Institute, a local high school.

"Yeh, well times have changed. Go to school." Then he leaned back, pulled himself up straight and said quite firmly: "But don't take any goddamned journalism. Get an education, if you can." He raised his hand in adieu or silent benediction.

My intrusion, I sensed, had come to a good stopping point.

"Thanks a lot, Mr. Mencken," I said and left.

I returned to the newsroom, passing Mr. Dorsey's desk. He glanced up at me. "That's it?"

"Yes, sir. Thanks."

"You didn't ask him to autograph any books, did you?"

"No, I didn't."

"That was wise. Now, let's get to work."

Only later did it occur to me that I had not even introduced myself. But that did not matter a great deal, I suspect. Mencken nodded the one other time I ever saw him.

"Hello, youngster. Go to school."

Eventually, thanks to the benefits of the GI Bill for Korea veterans, I managed to get that education. I also followed the advice of "The Sage of Baltimore"–worked on the school newspaper, was a "stringer" for the Associated Press, and served time with the *News-Post* and the Washington *Times Herald* and later, the *National Journal*–but never took a minute of Journalism in my life. One of my English instructors, Carl Bode, knew a great deal about Mencken himself, but that is another story altogether.

Perhaps times have changed with regard to the benefits of Journalism courses and Mencken's narrow viewpoint toward that academic discipline was undoubtedly biased. But to my recollection, Dr. Bode never advised any of his students to seek Journalism courses.

Whatever his many prejudices, Mencken was clearly right about newspapering—he would have scoffed at the title of journalist as pretentious—it is, he wrote, "the maddest, gladdest, damndest existence ever enjoyed."

REFERENCES ———————————————————

Russell Baker, *The Good Times* (New York: William Morrow, 1989).

Francis E. Beirne, *The Amiable Baltimoreans* (Baltimore: Johns Hopkins University Press, 1984).

H.L. Mencken, *H.L. Mencken's Days: Happy Days, Newspaper Days, Heathen Days* (New York: Dorset, 1989).

———, "Mencken's Baltimore," John Dorsey, ed. *The Sunday Sun* [8 September 1974] 1:39.

———, *Treatise on the Gods* (New York: Knopf, 1930/Johns Hopkins University Press, 1996).

Harold A. Williams, *The Baltimore Sun: 1837-1987* (Baltimore: Johns Hopkins University Press, 1987).

Chapter Two

Money Matters

MONEY MATTERED A GREAT DEAL to H. L. Mencken. Extensive, if not exhaustive, comments concerning fiduciary affairs figure prominently in his personal papers and diaries. Human nature prompts everyone to curiosity about other people's finances, and abundant evidence in print and unpublished records provides a deeper understanding of the man. This fiscal information reveals Mencken's world and a gives a clearer portrait of his character.

Mencken's partial autobiography can be gleaned from his books–*Happy Days*, 1880-1892 [1940]; *Newspaper Days*, 1899-1906 [1941]; *Heathen Days*, 1890-1936 [1943]–and several biographies are excellent–Manchester [1950], Bode [1969] and Fitzpatrick [1989]. After Mencken's papers were released by the Enoch Pratt, additional information emerged that reveals the private Mencken: Hobson's *Mencken: A Life* [1994] benefits from those sources. Later, Mencken's posthumous works edited by others–*The Diary of H. L. Mencken* [1989]; *My Life as Author and Editor* [1993]; and *Thirty-five Years of Newspaper Work* [1994]–provide more insight. One clear thread through Mencken's life was his concern for and concentration on monetary affairs. But detailed fiscal data not germane to the narratives in the books cited are omitted. Much of that information, the warp and woof of Mencken's interest, is provided here.

For the most part, Mencken's early years were secure and even happy, he writes. From 1880 until 1900, his outlook on the future and expectations for growth paralleled the nation itself: prosperous and self-confident, insular and self-indulgent, optimistic and self-satisfied. Mencken's family was not rich, but its status was well-placed above most in Baltimore. His father was a successful businessman, a dealer in wholesale tobacco and manufacturer of cigars. Young Mencken was born September 1880, in a house on Lexington Street near Fremont. In 1884, for $2,900, his father bought a new house near Union Square at 352 (now 1524) Hollins Street where Henry lived for most of his life. A year later, Mencken's father purchased a four-story warehouse on Paca Street for $15,000. He was also a part-owner of the Washington, D. C. Baseball Club. In 1891 he bought a summer home in Mt. Washington, a well-to-do neighborhood in northwest Baltimore, with four acres of land for $3,000. [A factor of twenty acquaints contemporary readers with dollar sums comparable to today's value.] The elder Mencken was a man of substantial means who advocated a doctrine of not incurring debt and staunchly opposed an eight-hour work day, doctrines that young Mencken embraced for the rest of his life. The panic of 1892-93 (where America witnessed its President appeal to banker J.P. Morgan to save the government) and a warehouse fire in December brought dark days but no financial disaster to the Mencken household. Mencken grew up in an insular and prosperous Baltimore, a realm he was to revisit affectionately in print a half-century later, with no money worries to trouble him. He led a privileged life, a boy with a pony and trap who responded with remote and benign indifference to the gritty poverty that was clear to see. With his books for guidance, Mencken's life was an ordered and contented existence and if he was aware of the stark bleakness in Baltimore, he was blithely free from any of its harsh realities.

He was spared attending public grammar schools– Baltimore in that era boasted one of the best–and a private academy prepared him for high school. He completed high school at the Baltimore Polytechnic Institute in 1896, with a $100 graduation present from his father for finishing first in his class. Young Harry went to work for his father that same year for $3.00 a week as a cigar salesman. (The average wage at that time was $450 annually; unskilled laborers averaged $300.) Mencken started at the bottom of the scale. His wages were spending money, however, not the stuff of existence. He met little success as a salesman, but his aptitude for writing showed promise and evenings and off-hours were devoted to writing and reading.

In 1900, HLM records his first income as an author–$15 from *Short Stories.* Some half dozen other sales followed through 1903. In 1901, *Frank Leslie's Popular Monthly* paid him $50 for a short story and later he declined a job as an editor. Mencken had no desire to leave Baltimore, then or ever.

His father's death freed Mencken to pursue the newspaper career he sought and, since his father died intestate, endowed him a portion of the estate and co-owner of the Hollins Street house. Later, Mencken would admit with wry humor that he "had the misfortune that my father was relatively well-off." Thus, unencumbered by family financial obligations, Mencken sought a newspaper post. He haunted the offices of the *Morning Herald* for months until he was taken on. Industrious, and with a sense of family obligation, Mencken continued at both jobs, day and night, for six months.

Even so, his first newspaper salary, in July 1899, while an improvement, was less than a living wage; the *Morning Herald* paid him $7.00 weekly to start. Comfortable circumstances enabled him to take employment at a low wage, an advantage over others no less ambitious. He was a diligent worker undaunted by long and demanding hours. Mencken did not consider college. "I am much too vain to have regrets," he recalled years later. Princeton was the favorite academic choice of Baltimore's upper-level elite, then and today. But Mencken more than met the competition from college-educated coworkers through diligence: "I was willing to work." This was his lifelong credo. Before the year was out, Mencken was earning $10 weekly.

Unquestionably, Mencken was an indefatigable worker who demonstrated uncommon promise. He often worked 12-hour days. Additionally, he continued to pursue free-lance writing. By the next year he was earning $14, then $16, then $18 weekly from his newspaper job. Promotion, to city editor, came in 1903, then managing editor two years later. Mencken was an able reporter and a resourceful manager–a "company man"–who did not hesitate to weed out poor performers and reduce staff to cut

costs for his employers. He confessed years later that he sometimes fired someone out of simple dislike.

At 21, Mencken, increasingly solvent, transferred to his
mother his portion of his father's bequest. His diligence added
to his independence. By 1902 he was free-lancing for the
Philadelphia *Inquirer* and other newspapers and by 1904 was
earning $30 weekly from short stories. In 1904 the great
Baltimore fire saw editor Mencken exert extraordinary energies,
administrative as well as editorial, to keep his paper going
despite being burned out. The performance helped enhance his
reputation as a "boy wonder." Mencken himself helped perpe-
trate the myth that he did not sleep for three days. Early on,
Mencken proved to be an apt student of self-promotion and public relations, a quality he found objectionable in others.

After the *Herald* folded ("sold down the river," Mencken
said), he joined the Baltimore *News* in 1906 as news editor at
$40 weekly, then six months later he moved to Baltimore's para-
mount newspaper the *Sun,* as Sunday editor. This elevation saw
Mencken acquire shares of *Sunpaper* stock as he moved into
management. His free-lance fiction earned him $75 a story from
Red Book. Mencken recalled that he "worked all the time" and
routinely put in 10-and 12-hour days. The break that gave
Mencken a national pulpit came in 1908. He became literary
reviewer, at $50 monthly, for the New York City-based *Smart
Set,* "A Magazine of Cleverness," another free-lance literary
enterprise that augmented his regular newspaper salary. He
made his first appearance in November in a column signed
"Henry L. Mencken." The familiar shortened version came several months later. He landed the job largely on the recommen-
dation of a Baltimore newspaper acquaintance, mistakenly concluded by Mencken to be Channing Pollack. Mencken's literary
credentials were largely based on his three books–*Ventures into
Verse* [1903], *George Bernard Shaw: His Plays* [1905], and *The
Philosophy of Friedrich Nietzsche* [1908]. These works won
Mencken a growing reputation but no income. Later, as more
lucrative outlets beckoned, he could be ingenuous, as Yardley
observes, if not dishonest, in wriggling out of a publisher's agree-
ment. Above all, Mencken was a canny man of business.

Financially, he was doing well, earning more than $1,000 a

year. At the *Sunpapers,* he received a $3.00 a week raise and was promoted to assistant editorial writer. But from 1908 on, he carefully noted, his free-lance income exceeded his salaried position. A dollar bought a great deal in those days. A solid gold hunter case watch could be had for $4.95; $29.95 bought a 100-piece place setting of imported Haviland Limoges china. Mencken did well enough to sail Britain's White Star Line for his first European trip in that year. Mencken was prospering, without question. His recognition of self-promotion prompted him to engage a clipping service to keep track of his mentions and publication citations.

Thus, before he was thirty Mencken had achieved financial independence with a solid source of income from his newspaper salary augmented by healthy infusions from free-lance work. He was not burdened with the obligation of most working men to provide food and lodging for himself; remained at Hollins Street. He had neither wife nor family to support; he contributed a portion of his earnings to the family expenses that were minimal in a modest Baltimore neighborhood. He walked to work or took a trolley to Sun Square, a few blocks distant.

Increasing opportunities opened up as Mencken avidly pursued people and outlets for his writing. Theodore Dreiser, then editor of the *Delineator,* paid Mencken $125 each for two articles but Mencken declined an offer to join the magazine (for $50 a month). His next book, a joint venture, *Man vs. The Men,* [1909] was a commercial failure, but Mencken could afford to write books primarily to build his literary reputation despite a negligible income. Mencken was not chained to an office with regular hours; he wrote his newspaper columns and was free to devote time to magazine chores in New York. At home he diligently attended to his correspondence (through his lifetime letters were answered in a day or two), editing and writing, usually until 10 p.m. nightly, only then allowing time for recreation. Mencken was blessed with abundant energy and a capacity for work. Work, he admitted, was his recreation.

By 1913, his income totalled $4,645.48; income from the *Smart Set* alone amounted to $1,750 and investment from bonds paid $140. This was a considerable increase from 1912's $962.50. His monthly stipend from the *Smart Set* was now

$100. The new federal income tax, introduced by a provision in President Woodrow Wilson's tariff act, was modest: only one per cent on incomes up to $20,000. By September 1914, Mencken reached the post he had been striving for: co-editor of the *Smart Set,* with fellow staffer George Jean Nathan. Nathan, originally offered the position, accepted only with Mencken in tandem, not so much for his literary talent but for his business acumen. Once in charge, Mencken found ways to cut costs, firing staff and instituting overhead reductions. One of the editors jettisoned was Norman Boyer, a former newspaper friend from Baltimore and the man responsible for originally bringing Mencken aboard (unknown to Mencken). Nevertheless, Boyer's subsequent suicide was callously dismissed by Mencken, who described him as "a foolish fellow." It was an outlook prompted in part by Mencken's hard business side that had dealt with other dismissals in similar fashion. As editor, he came aboard with a 1/6 ownership of stock and a monthly salary of $150. Mencken's income was $6,218.46 for 1914. His fortunes were improving.

Elsewhere in America, Henry Ford created a sensation when he announced the eight-hour, $5.00 a day rate for his automobile workers, creating wage and hour standards largely unmet by American industry. In 1914 another joint venture book, *Europe After 8.15,* ill-timed with Europe ablaze, met with financial failure, but Mencken's real reward was an increasing literary recognition. To help the financial health of the magazine, however, Mencken himself made overtures to potential advertisers, but he was no more successful with ad sales than he had been with cigars twenty years before.

In 1916 Mencken published his fourth book, *A Book of Burlesques,* whose total royalties over the next three years yielded only $96.68. In the same year he produced the *Little Book in C Major* that did worse, $44.25. Mencken began to think about another publisher.

With the Great War coming closer to America, Mencken defended the German sinking of the *Lusitania,* reasoning that the ship carried contraband munitions. Mencken's commentary caused him to be referred to in Baltimore as a "krauthead" and his pro-German pieces lost him "The Free Lance" column in the *Evening Sun.* Baltimore was, in fact, a large German center and the language was spoken in many of its public schools. War fever and public outrage, however, was impossible to ignore; the newspaper's proprietors reluctantly decided that Mencken's column had to go. But his work was now appearing in broader forums, the *Atlantic Monthly,* for example. Meanwhile, he continued his magazine work in New York and studiously avoided any mention of the war in the *Smart Set.*

He and Nathan had set up, on the side, two pulp magazines featuring hack writers–*Parisienne* and *Saucy Stories*–that took a minimum of effort. Mencken was able to use his employer's facilities in these enterprises with little threat of loss, other than his time. The lucrative "louse" magazines (Mencken's description) used less-talented authors, changed story locales to Paris (from submissions rejected by the *Smart Set*), required little work and sold well. In October 1916, Mencken, dickering for himself and Nathan, managed to sell their shares for $10,000 each, a windfall of unexpected bounty for a modest enterprise.

His link and income with the *Sunpapers* was not totally lost. In December 1916, the newspaper commissioned him as war correspondent. He sailed for Europe to cover the "German situation" and progress of the war. Prudently, in a side business venture, Mencken also arranged to file dispatches for the Wheeler Newspaper Features (soon the Bell Syndicate) as Mencken's income entries disclose another source of income. In April 1917, Mencken resorted to the pro German *New York Evening Mail* as an outlet for his newspaper work. After a year his income from that source alone amounted to $2,155. The *Mail* was a convenient outlet; his famous bathtub hoax appeared in its pages before the newspaper was shut down by the Wilson Administration.

Mencken needed newspapers as an outlet. His money making formula was simple: get paid three times for an idea, first as a newspaper piece, then reworked as a magazine article and finally, in book form. This was the structure followed in *A Book of Prefaces,* his first book published by Alfred A. Knopf. Its royalties earned $108.67 in 1918 and $78.48 the next year. Material from newspaper and magazine origins went into his next book ventures, *Damn! A Book of Calumny* and *In Defense of Women.* Both were unprofitable despite his efforts to explore new methods of display and advertising. Mencken was better at marketing himself than his books. The *Smart Set's* "Pistols for Two" pamphlet, with Nathan, yielded negligible royalties that failed to meet costs but helped gain notoriety. Greater success came with *Prejudices: First Series* and significant royalties, $335.60 in 1919. Again, he acknowledged, the indirect benefits were enormous. All told, Mencken received $1,863.73 until the book went out of print in 1933. A series of *Prejudices* followed, each profitable ventures.

As editors, he and Nathan came up with a personal money-making device. However often the editors' salaries were delayed (at times payment was withheld for months), they always insisted on, and collected, $100 as authors' fees for any written piece for the *Smart Set,* as was any other contributing writer. A great portion of the magazine was, in fact, written by the two editors under various pseudonyms. Mencken freely acknowledged that this work would not have been accepted or printed anywhere else, but it was an avenue to ready money. Authors were paid promptly by the magazine. Mencken was acutely aware that appearance counted: "it pays to be thought rich," he observed. He was not above inflating figures for public consumption, a device he found odious in others.

Mencken worked diligently to escape wartime service of any kind, and exerted significant efforts to remain uninvolved in war work in any capacity. His most ambitious book, *The American Language,* produced royalties of $593.30 in 1919. This and subsequent editions were to prove the most lucrative of Mencken's enterprises. The rights for a play written with Nathan, *Heliogabalus,* yielded $343.

By January 1920, Mencken was again back on the *Sunpaper* payroll at $50 weekly, resuming his regular weekly column which normally ran on Monday but could just as likely show up on a Saturday. On January 1st Mencken recorded that his income was $3,000 a year. The Twenties were epochal for Mencken. In 1921, he managed to sell shares of yet another of the most successful of the pulp magazines that he and Nathan had concocted, *Black Mask,* for $20,000, an enterprise that Mencken admitted made him $25,000 in two years.

From this point on in his career, Mencken worked from a

solid base of financial security. In effect, he was no longer depen-
dent on a salaried income to sustain him. He joined the *Nation*
as a contributing editor; this added trifling income but some
prestige (he dropped the post in 1932). More important, he left
the *Smart Set* in 1923 to mine other, more profitable sources of
income; a new magazine venture, financed by Knopf.

On January 1, 1924, he was appointed co-editor of the
American Mercury with a 1/6 share of stock and a salary of $100
monthly. Nathan came along, but Mencken was the senior part-
ner, entrusted with the business side of the enterprise. He hired
staff, leased office space and managed work arrangements.
Mencken signed a contract in 1925 to write a weekly column for
the *Chicago Tribune* and its syndicate at $200 an essay, gener-
ated in part as a result of the national fame his dispatches created from the 1924 Scopes trial in Dayton, Tennessee. This event
became a sensational news event that Mencken in large measure
engineered with the resources of the *Evening Sun*. By the end
of 1924 Mencken had also inherited all of his parents' holdings
under the terms of his mother's will.

Mencken's financial ledgers show that in 1928 income from
the *Sunpapers* amounted to $5,000.04 in salary and $1,935 in
dividends; $9,000 from the *American Mercury* in salary and
$1,250 in dividends; $5,262.96 in royalties and $2,048.20 from
Knopf dividends; $800 from the Tribune Syndicate; $100 from
the Bell Syndicate; and, he carefully noted, $2.00 from the
Nation. On that total of $25,398.20, he paid $660.60 income
tax. Financially, Mencken was soaring in rare company; only 2.3
per cent of American families had an income of $10,000; less
than eight per cent had an income of $5,000.

The Wall Street Crash of 1929 did little damage to Mencken
financially; he was too prudent to indulge in the frenzied margin
buying that helped bring about that financial debacle. Further,
he wrote that the event was "no surprise" and he had seen it
coming. His stocks, like everyone else's, lost value–his AT&T
dropped from 304 to 197 1/4, General Motors from 72 3/4 to 36,
and Montgomery Ward 137 7/8 to 49 1/4. But Mencken held on
unfazed. For him, the Great Depression was merely another
cyclical financial episode much like those he had experienced in
1892 and 1907.

He failed to recognize the Great Depression for the calamity that it was. The story of Mencken in New York, confronting a lineup at soup kitchens with dismay is no doubt accurate, but reveals a Mencken almost coldly indifferent to the plight of the masses without jobs or prospects. Perhaps Mencken was too insulated from the common working world. Perhaps he embraced the Horatio Alger, Jr. myth: "[T]here are few places where an industrious man cannot get a living, if he is willing to accept such work as falls his way." This may explain his attitude toward his brother Charlie, who lost his railroad job and needed help through the Depression. Henry, prosperous though he was, gave assistance grudgingly and sporadically; he never doubted that if any man wanted a job he could get one.

Mencken's failure to recognize that the Great Depression was a watershed in the American experience contributed to a waning of his popularity and the eventual demise of his writing in the *Mercury;* he simply lost touch with the temper of the times and his ideas lost coinage.

In the 1930s Mencken's income declined slightly, but he was by no means in dire straits. His *Sunpaper* salary continued at the same level, which he meticulously recorded each month at $416.67 for its yearly total of $5,000.04; his newspaper dividends that year actually increased to $2,580. Knopf book dividends fell to $292; but Mencken's royalties increased to $6,394.28, and the *American Mercury* salary continued at $9,000 for a total of $23,266.32. His income tax rose to $872.36, perhaps another reason to despise FDR's New Deal. He consented to join the board of directors of the A.S. Abell Co., owners and proprietors of the *Sunpapers.* In 1932 he joined the board of directors of Alfred A. Knopf, Inc., holding 250 shares of preferred and 50 shares of common stock. He used that forum to continue to air his personal views to deny advance royalties to authors (which he himself always refused), a stance not endorsed by his fellow directors or Knopf.

Mencken was careful with money. He prudently sold his unwanted book review copies to a Baltimore dealer. Before the 1933 "Bank Holiday," he had, on a tip, quietly extracted an ample amount of cash to get by during those tight times. In Baltimore, Sparrows Point steel workers were paid 18.5 cents an hour in 1938–$5.80 a week. In 1932, Mencken's *Making a President*, a collection of *Evening Sun* convention dispatches, failed as a money-maker (royalties were $344.30) and Mencken called it his worst book. In the mid-30s Mencken's *Sunpapers* salary rose to $1,000 monthly, his *American Mercury* salary disappeared in 1933 with his departure as editor, but he earned dividends from Knopf and *Sun* stock as well as quarterly payments from more than 58 blue-chip stocks and bonds.

After his marriage in 1930 to Sara Powell Haardt, Mencken moved to an apartment at 307 Cathedral Street, near Mt. Vernon Place, a neighborhood far more up-scale than Hollins Street. He and Sara maintained separate accounts. Tubercular, Sara died in May 1935 and Mencken was devastated. He arranged her papers for placement at Baltimore's Goucher College, where she had been a student and faculty member, arranged for a publisher of her collected stories, *Southern Album.* He sent copies to college and university libraries with his personal card. In his accounts, Mencken dutifully noted a contribution of $2.00 to the annual Christmas TB campaign, apparently without irony.

Mencken was not a large contributor to charities, according to his listings for income tax deductions–less than $200, with $100 of that for the American Friends Service and eight of the ten or so contributions to German-related service organizations. He continued to faithfully contribute $2.00 for the TB campaign each year, however.

Shortly after Sara's death, Mencken declined an offer of $10,000 to write a series of five articles on contemporary American life in order to concentrate his time and attention on a new edition of *The American Language.* Acquisition of capital was not a major impetus; he was well fixed financially, with no pressing need to acquire more. His resources were more than ample; the book would assure a more lasting provision. In 1936 the new edition yielded him $7,001.23 in royalties and in 1937, $5,814.20.

By 1936, Mencken had returned to Hollins Street and income for that year topped $20,000. He provided support to his younger brother, in and out of work because of the hard economic times, and assisted his niece, Virginia, with college funds. Mencken, however, spent more–$2,700 to bind his records and clippings and in 1937 and 1938 sent 89 of these volumes to the Enoch Pratt Free Library, the first of many hundreds he was to supply to display his manuscripts and letters. Mencken was not ungenerous but he adamantly refused to recognize the pervasive and eroding effects of the Great Depression, fought the New Deal and venomously opposed President Franklin D. Roosevelt personally. Later, it would get worse when FDR proclaimed in 1942, that "No American citizen ought to have a net income, after he has paid his taxes, of more than $25,000 a year."

One writing project that Mencken turned to with enthusiasm was a *History of the Sunpapers* [1937] that he shared with three colleagues. This book paid no royalties. It was a monumental work, but here Mencken the historian, was too much the company man. He proved to be selective and distasteful facts were simply passed over or omitted, a trait for which in the past he had castigated others.

In 1938 Mencken returned to the news room full-time to supervise revamping of the *Evening Sun's* editorial page. He threw himself into the project with single-minded purpose and succeeded in driving nearly everyone crazy. His mark was left everywhere and often he felt the need to write every editorial and his influence is evident. Practically no one measured up to his expectations, so the burden fell on him. Mencken was simply incapable of delegation. He worked day and night. The experience drove him, he admits, to "near paranoia," and lasted less than six months. It was his last foray into active newspaper work.

By the 1940s Mencken had resigned from the *Sunpapers* following the cancellation of his Monday column, again for his outspoken pro-German, anti-English stance. Mencken forever saw this as an abrogation of Free Speech, forgetting that publishers have the prerogative to publish what the hired help writes. Ironically, Mencken saw no parallel when as editor, he had denied the newspaper's editorial pages to colleagues like Gerald W. Johnson, once an old friend, whom he now viewed as too liberal in outlook and a New Deal zealot.

In 1943 Mencken's income was $19,627.34, with $2,675 from various writings–*Esquire, New Yorker, Saturday Evening Post* and the *Reader's Digest*–his *Sunpaper* salary and dividends, $10,893.81; Knopf dividends, directors fees and royalties,

$12,295.71; and $4,053.86 from stock dividends, all blue-chip steady payers. His writing income was dwarfed by "outside" revenue, a point which gave Mencken especial pleasure.

By 1944, Mencken's weekly salary had been reduced from $12,000 annually to $9,000, and he virtually ceased writing chores for the newspaper. Mencken retained his ties to the *Sunpapers* as a member of the Board of Directors. He lectured at Columbia University at $250 each for five appearances. Four articles for the *Reader's Digest* paid $2,500. His writing turned to reminiscences, that promised to be perhaps his most-read. Four articles for the *New Yorker,* at editor Harold Ross's urging (for which he was paid from $230 to $300 each), led to the first of the *Days* books. *Happy Days* appeared in 1940 and sold more than 10,000 copies in the first five months and earned him $3.782.97 in royalties. *Newspaper Days* in 1941 brought in $2,584.86. Income for the year was $24,450 (a quarter-million dollars in 1990s purchasing power). In 1942 his income reached $23,500 with publication of his massive *Dictionary of Quotations* and by 1943, with publication of *Heathen Days,* Mencken calculated his net worth as $185,000.

Mencken performed fewer chores for the *Sunpapers,* but one task he undertook was to handle management's negotiations with the Newspaper Guild. He professed to be in favor of the Guild but felt it had fallen under suspect leadership. He saw it as "a conspiracy of the incompetent against the boss and the good men." The Guild's goal of a 40-hour week remained anathema, as passed on by his father and strengthened by experience. His view echoed that of a half-century earlier. Of newspapers, Mencken said: "you can no more have a 40-hour week for a good reporter than for an archbishop." Mencken proved to be a poor negotiator and removed himself from the bargaining table before the Guild settled its contract. Mencken's intransigence helped prompt the strike that finally won the Guild its demands.

Mencken further loosened his ties with the newspaper. He requested that publisher Paul Patterson reduce his *Sunpaper* salary to allow him to write for other newspapers. His ledgers, nevertheless, record a continuing *Sunpaper* salary of $700 monthly, or $8,400 annually, until 1948 when it was further reduced to $416.67 monthly. That was the year Mencken made his last major appearance for the newspaper, covering the three major political conventions in Philadelphia.

Through the 1940s, Mencken's royalties from Knopf, mainly for *The American Language,* amounted to $4,021.57 in 1944; $6,469.61 in 1945; $16,965.93 in 1946; $7,785.22 in 1947; and $8,180.65 through October 1948, when his notations ceased.

Following the war, Mencken helped sustain many friends and relatives in Germany with CARE packages, each recipient and cost recorded carefully in his ledger with Teutonic exactitude.

Mencken had one last adventure as a working newspaperman. The presidential nominating conventions of 1948, as Cooke records, displayed Mencken as he once was, reveling in the glory of political newspaper reporting. It was his last work as a reporter on deadline, working from the press gallery and meeting with the politicians that he respected, the scoundrels of machine politics, and his final brush with those he loathed, the do-good reformers. He suspected it might be his last big story, as he promised to "become an angel soon."

His writing and his personal ledger entries ceased the month before his stroke in 1948. It was a tragedy–Mencken could no longer read or write–especially for a man whose personal sense of relaxation was work. He was forced to watch television, which he loathed as "terrible" and a contribution to "the American libido for the hideous." In February 1950, Mencken was awarded a *Sunpaper* pension of $7,500 annually. Not until April 1949 did Mencken formally resign from the Knopf board of directors.

He left a $300,000 estate when he died in 1956. Brother August and sister Gertrude were provided for and he left $10,000 to his secretary and "more modest" sums to his housekeeper and to his brother Charles and his wife and daughter. Three quarters of the remainder of the $300,000 estate went to the Enoch Pratt Library and one quarter to the Johns Hopkins Hospital. Thus, much of the money that Mencken accumulated through a lifetime continues to inform the world that he lived and contributed much. The major portion of Mencken's legacy was to assure his own literary immortality.

Jacob Marley was condemned in death to carry a ponderous clanking chain of ledgers, cash boxes, keys, and account books. H. L. Mencken metaphorically did so in life. In his compulsive attention to all matters financial, important and trivial, Mencken, as Yardley noted, "goes beyond the pale" and his financial accounting "cites not merely chapter and verse but line and syllable as well." Mencken's reckonings, noted month by month, year by year and carried out to exacting detail, surely consumed a large portion of each day crowded with writing, editing, and correspondence. Accounts of monies spent and earned occupied his mind. He kept meticulous accounts of petty expenses–typewriter ribbons, push-pins, scratch pads and laundry bills (an average of $6.20 a month over one year). Exact detail of such arcane trivia–all entries made by his own hand and not delegated elsewhere–were noted daily.

Beyond the reckoning of numbers, Mencken's business dealings, petty deceits and prevaricating maneuvers reveal a human heart laid bare with all its faults. Mencken followed a strict code of honor as he saw it and did not lie outright, but he did not necessarily tell the truth. He was not above evasive and elliptical reasoning to justify dubious actions, personal and otherwise; he had the mind of a Jesuit at times. He frequently displayed commendable generosity but could be niggardly to those closest to him. He could be caring and considerate, but was often impervious to the effect his brusque actions had on those of lesser talent. He was blandly indifferent to the adversities inflicted on others by fortune that they, unlike himself, failed to master.

Mencken was a paradox. The genius and vitality of his writing endures on its merits and requires, for those with wit and humor, no apology for content or point of view. Behind it all, and perhaps critical to understanding H. L. Mencken the man, is the motivation revealed by his account books. His was a consuming desire for the smug gratification, satisfaction, and superiority that comes from debts fully paid, and the protective security of an ample bank account. This was Mencken's constant, life-long preoccupation.

REFERENCES

Carl Bode, *Mencken* (Baltimore: Johns Hopkins University Press, 1986).

Vincent Fitzpatrick, *H.L. Mencken* (New York: Unger/Continuum, 1989).

Fred Hobson, *Mencken: A Life* (New York: Random House, 1994).

William L. Manchester, *Disturber of the Peace: The Life of H.L. Mencken* (New York: Harper, 1950).

H.L. Mencken, *My Life As Author and Editor*, Jonathan Yardley, ed. (New York: Knopf, 1993/Vintage, 1995).

_____, *The Diary of H.L. Mencken*, Charles A. Fecher, ed. (New York: Knopf, 1989/Vintage, 1991).

_____, *Thirty-five Years of Newspaper Work*, Fred Hobson, Vincent Fitzpatrick and Bradford Jacobs, eds. (Baltimore: Johns Hopkins University Press, 1994).

H.L. Mencken Room, Enoch Pratt Free Library of Baltimore, Md., selected papers.

Sam Pizzigati, "Salary Caps for Everyone!," *The New York Times* [28 August 1994] E15.

Chapter Three

Prejudice Without Discrimination

PUBLICATION OF HIS PRIVATE DIARY resurrected charges that H. L. Mencken was an anti-Semite. Judged narrowly by today's standards of politically correct behavior, he was. Mencken, dead for more than forty years, retains the power to stir violent passions, as he did in his lifetime. His literary production was monumental, and Mencken continues to add to his work with publication of his collected papers. Clearly, Walter Lippmann's assessment in the 1920s that HLM "was the most powerful personal influence on this whole generation of educated people" applies to later generations as well. Mencken's acerbic polemics retain a vigor that shocks a reading public imbued with non-confrontational "political correctness." Mencken was opinionated, obtuse, unbending, and unyielding. His writings, combined with mischievous humor of deadly design, bring to life men and events forgotten. But a narrow bigot Mencken was not.

His private diary discloses that Mencken harbored thoughts unpopular today. His closest biographer Manchester, noted that Mencken "expressly prohibited" publication of the diary in his will. Nevertheless, the Enoch Pratt Free Library of Baltimore, custodians of many HLM papers, aided with a favorable ruling by the State of Maryland Attorney General, allowed publication of large portions of the diary that brought to light his personal prejudices and opinions. Few of his private thoughts, however, were at odds with Mencken's published work.

The resultant furor raises questions of how many of HLM's present critics have actually read his works. His diary employs expletives and opinions that appeared in print any number of times. In life, "the Disturber of the Peace" relished nothing more than to "stir up the animals" and to his delight, Mencken was regularly attacked through his career. Indeed, he eagerly collected and gleefully published the brickbats in *Menckeniana: A Schimpflexikon* [1928]. He would have particularly enjoyed the fervor in the National Press Club (which he disdained) where zealots purged the Library of his name because of his prejudices. Mencken would undoubtedly note that the ruckus proved his point precisely.

Many in today's audience have never heard of "The Sage of Baltimore," a great newspaperman surely. This includes many journalism students, blissfully unaware of his work or his contributions. One leading textbook fails to even mention Mencken. This would not have surprised Mencken, for he held most academicians in low esteem. Perhaps like Mark Twain before him, Mencken's stature requires reappraisal. Twain was not the lighthearted, humorous lightweight originally reckoned. Indeed, Mencken thumped for Twain's rightful place in American literature and stoutly championed *The Adventures of Huckleberry Finn* as the greatest American novel, whatever its flaws. The controversy over Huck's companion, Nigger Jim, would have made Mencken howl (the bulwark of the First Amendment fails protection of usage of the word "nigger," as modern dictionaries undergo change).

Mencken's newspaper work came early in the century and he quickly made a mark above the general level. Mencken's aim, he explained, was "to combat, chiefly by ridicule, American piety, stupidity, tin-pot moralism, cheap chauvinism in all their forms." Nothing was sacred. But with all the slinging of dead cats, Mencken managed to bring an intellectual stature to newspaper writing, achieved by Lippmann, Heywood Broun, and later perhaps by James Reston. Bode and Rodgers have collected examples of Mencken's sparkling, out-spoken, opinionated newspaper prose and his descriptions castigated virtually every politician in America.

Mencken's literary flowering emerged with the national forum provided him through the *Smart Set* (1908-23) and the *American Mercury* (1925-33), where he influenced a generation of writers. For more than two decades these two magazines displayed Mencken's literary voice—vitriol unsurpassed, startling and sardonic—reflecting his own peculiar views of American life and letters. He reminded readers that George Washington, a drinker, profane, land-grabbing money grubber who regarded the common people as inflammatory dolts, would stand little chance of election in modern times. Nolte writes that Mencken was perhaps no Swift, no Voltaire, but "the nearest thing to these giants that America has ever produced."

Through his magazines Mencken was instrumental in developing talented writers and bringing the best foreign writers to the attention of readers. During his reign at the *American Mercury* Mencken became one of America's most influential magazine editors; his was not the vast audience of the *Saturday Evening Post* or even of the *Atlantic,* but the intellectual—an elite group. His critical contribution was significant in providing a favorable climate for the growth of national letters. All the while, Mencken battled with the academicians, who were he noted, "as timid and flatulent as a journalist." Mencken "was hated and feared," writes Nolte, "more than any other American of his day by the average university teacher." Nevertheless, Mencken helped propel American letters to the first rank.

Mencken's language of acrimony made his commentary pungent. The average citizen of democracy was nothing more than "a goose-stepping ignoramus" and worse. HLM was even harder on presidents: Harding was "stupid," "cowardly" and a "numskull"; Coolidge "puerile"; Hoover would "have made a good bishop." Mencken saved his most savage attacks for FDR, a "thief" was one of the least offensive. Mencken viewed these and other similar comments as "constructive criticism."

Mencken made two major contributions to American literature through the *Mercury* and his books: he attacked with vigor and venom the crippling virus of Puritanism and he provided support for writers of realism—such as Drieser, Willa Cather, Sinclair Lewis, and others. His successful battle for realism ranks as a notable achievement in American thought. His own books became vehicles for further comment, notably, *A Book of Prefaces* [1917], *Damn! A Book of Calumny* [1918] and *In Defense of Women* [1918], which some people interpret as a defense of women. From 1919 through 1927, the successive series of *Prejudices* represent Mencken at the peak of his influence, as James T. Farrell notes, with some of his wittiest, most buoyant, and deadliest writing.

Perhaps his greatest contribution was *The American Language* [1919] and it remains a classic with four editions, sixteen printings and two supplements. Described as a "Declaration of Independence" for the American language, the work had a profound effect on American writers; it is a work of scholarship, opinionated, humorous and highly readable. One wonders what Mencken would have made of psychobabble and the grotesque convolutions wrought by politically correct constructions in common usage today, including "waitperson," "Congresspeople" and the awkward he/she tropism.

Modern euphemisms, ostensibly to enhance self-esteem and protect sensibilities, sharpen the contrast between Mencken's rigorous English usage and flaccid contemporary efforts to create a kinder and gentler world that makes mush of meaning. For example, the honest word "cripple" has yielded successively to "impaired," then "disabled," only to became "handicapped." The currently correct usage, in today's lexicon, is "challenged." Hence, when really "caring" people speak and write, the blind are no longer blind but "visually challenged." Mencken the philologist would be amused; Mencken the careful writer would be outraged.

In his later years Mencken produced the series of essays that appeared in the *New Yorker* and were turned into his highly popular and readable autobiographies: *Happy Days* [1940], *Newspaper Days* [1941] and *Heathen Days* [1943]. The trilogy remains a joy to read for the language, the spirit of the time and for their sheer zest and charm. Readers are warned, however, that phrases that offend present sensibilities occur, and Mencken can play fast and loose with facts if truth obstructs a good story. The essays contain a good many "stretchers" that dismay the historian. Mencken's colleague, Frank R. Kent, took umbrage at the liberties contained in "A Girl from Red Lion, P.A.," and asked: "Henry, why do you tell lies like that?"

HLM replied, "Well, it made a good story, didn't it?"

For these and other incidents, critics like Alistair Cooke contend that Mencken's literary assessments may not stand up and that Mencken should be remembered as "an American humorist out of Mark Twain and a superb journalist out of nowhere." Nolte, Kazin and others have made the case for Mencken's literary acumen, but Mencken's humor can prove elusive. Many continue to accept the White House bathtub hoax as gospel. Mencken's humor was subtle. A number of critics believed then and continue to believe now that his subtle barbs in *In Defense of Women* were a forthright and prescient banner for feminists.

Unquestionably, however, Mencken was first and foremost a newspaperman. Whatever he did and whenever he did it, that was his trade and the title he liked best. His newspaper career began in 1899, and his first editor, Max Ways, helped discipline his style. From that background, Mencken devised a set of rules, still workable for any journalist: (1) get dates, ages, figures of all kinds accurately; (2) never trust a cop; (3) get your copy in early; and (4) be aware of the laws of libel.

Like many writers of good prose, he began by writing bad poetry. Some of these efforts gained publication because he put them into his column. But no foolishness was off limits. Despite his popularity however, when the United States stood on the verge of war, the *Sunpapers* cancelled the "Free Lance." Mencken, vehemently anti-English and outspokenly pro German, was forced to yield his column not without some bitterness. In his last "Free Lance," he wrote: "The truth that survives is the lie that is pleasantest to believe." Mencken saw this move by his publisher as an affront to his First Amendment rights. After a brief stint as a "war correspondent" where he continued to laud the Germans, Mencken left the *Sunpapers* and took up brief residence for the *New York Evening Mail,* where he turned out a series of essays, among them the famous bathtub hoax and "Sahara of the Bozart." Nevertheless, the *Mail* was eventually shut down by the Wilson Administration as a pro-German newspaper.

After the war Mencken returned to the *Sunpapers* and turned his attention to politics; he resumed another column, but

"Free Lance" was never resurrected. He covered every political convention as a working newspaperman through 1948. Mencken continued to write with gusto, applauding when appropriate but castigating with compelling clarity his disdain for the "cheap and tawdry." Mencken's views were always iconoclastic without apology.

With the 1930s and the onset of the Great Depression, Mencken's attacks against Democracy, against pomposity, against pretense, lost favor when unemployment, hunger, and homelessness became issues of grave concern, which he ignored. His newspaper columns continued, but his pulpit with the *American Mercury* was imperiled. He simply did not comprehend the calamity of the economic collapse. In his mind the Depression was an invention of the "charity racketeers" and the people on Fifth Avenue "were no good anyway." In his newspaper comments he used the Depression to castigate FDR for either doing too much or too little. Protracted invective against FDR's attempts to provide jobs, food, and shelter were not met with sympathy by Mencken's readers. Attacks against plutocrats failed. Mencken, in effect, ignored the Depression and derided efforts to alleviate the suffering. He lost his audience.

During World War II, Mencken was again forced to relinquish his regular *Sunpaper* column because of his continuing strong pro-German, anti-British writing. While clearly pro-German, Hitler was seen as a "clown" and an "imbecile," and the Nazis as "a gang of lunatics" who would soon be disposed by the German people. Mencken did not take Hitler seriously. He lost friends, particularly Jewish friends, over this issue and failed to understand why. Mencken saw the war in Europe as a British morass that would enmesh America. His Germany was the cultured world of Goethe and Bach. He despised the British and never forgave Woodrow Wilson for getting the nation into WWI. This elitist argument was lost on the few he cared to influence. Time passed Mencken by.

Present day witnesses who profess outrage at Mencken's biases are not alone. In 1948, the Progressive Party attempted to include in its platform a resolution that stated in part: "H. L. Mencken is guilty of Hitlerite references" and asserted that he "Red-baits, Jew-baits and Negro-baits" and otherwise committed

"un-American slander" (as opposed to American slander?).
Cooke writes that Mencken acknowledged its reading from the
press gallery with a slight bow. The resolution failed to pass.
Cooke, who asserted that Mencken was not a bigot of any kind,
notes that HLM complained about "the growing sensitiveness of
politicians" and commented that "nobody called me a white-
baiter" when he attacked Herbert Hoover. Times and sentiments
changed. Mencken did not.

Mencken's prose was scalding invective that assaulted all
institutions, people in high places and "boobs" of every stripe.
Wonderfully wicked, but without malice. He was an original,
humorous without wisecracks, extraordinarily accurate and dev-
astating. He was prejudiced without bias. Mencken attacked all
things–and everyone–that deserved censure. And in his view,
virtually all deserved it. He was wrong, often. But he held to
views formed early in life and seldom altered. Mencken was, of
course, anti-everything that displeased his view of the universe.
His steady pro-German position prevailed despite the fact that
he held a low opinion of most Germans, the "little Ottos."
Similarly, he held a low opinion of most Americans and democratic government. Nor did he hesitate to inform readers in terms
specific and unvarnished.

Mencken assaulted the inanities of society; he inveighed
against prophets and presidents without favor. He was an elitist
who dismissed the inferior mob. Latter-day critics who profess
dismay at Mencken's anti-Semitic language in his private diary
overlook the sweeping insults he hurled at all. If he was a bigot,
and by contemporary standards he surely was, one should not
single out his anti-Semitism.

Virtually every paragraph of Mencken's published writings,
much of which remains in print, is liberally sprinkled with an
astonishing variety of insults--racial, social and personal. If
Mencken was anti-Semitic (and he was not in public), others
fared no better. The Ku Klux Klan, which he regularly attacked
when it was a potent force in American politics, was in HLM's
estimation, an arm of the Methodist Church. Baptists and
Methodists were regularly referred to as "witch-burners." He
usually employed the term "pisbyterian bastards" but generally
shunned anti Roman Catholic sentiments. Christians in gener-

al, however, were dismissed as "the worst lice in creation."

Mencken wrote of the fundamentalist "Holy Rollers" and the religious fanaticism in the sense of an anthropologist dissecting the rites of an unknown civilization. Clearly, he no more believed in their activities than any of today's literate audience embrace Aztec or Druid ritual. He observed behavior he found bizarre and rendered harsh judgment.

Mencken followed a code of behavior acceptable in his level of society and therefore could write of the need for a "Mick," a "Dutchman," a "squarehead," a "dago," or a "guiney" to become "an American" without apology or condescension. For blacks–once in polite society termed Negroes–Mencken employed any number of terms to describe the race or individuals: smoke, coon, blackamoor, Aframericans (close to a more recently preferred terminology), Negro or when particularly waspish, cannibal. But "nigger" was rarely employed in his lexicon, personal or private. Mencken employed terms that were acceptable in his time and place. Was Mencken racist? Surely. He was elitist, unquestionably.

Was Mencken an anti-Semite? Not by his standards. For years a Jewish *Who's Who* listed Mencken. When asked why he did not correct the error, he responded: "Why should I correct it? What's wrong about it? Perhaps I am a Jew. Besides, it's kind of nice being known as a Jew. A lot of people might give me credit for more brains than I have." He, like many others then, and today, attributed peculiar characteristics to Jews. His mistake, apparently, was to say so in his private diary. Mencken also, to the shock of many readers today, assessed his fellow workers and colleague in harsh terms as his private papers reveal. Some colleagues with whom he worked closely he evaluated in hard, professional terms unpleasant to readers today. In fact, few people measured up to the standards that Mencken set and he said so. In none of these cases are the individuals Jews.

Measured by today's standards, Mencken was a bigot, and perhaps might be judged a hypocrite for maintaining good professional relations while privately finding individuals wanting. Any number of people failed that Mencken litmus. Mencken's environment and era regularly employed terms in disfavor today. His descriptions were invariably barbed, and society now frowns on such usage. Perhaps modern society suffers from a mass hypocrisy that Mencken surely would find amusing. Students no longer fail because they are lazy or, God forbid, lack intelligence–that is to say, are stupid. They are not motivated. Or perhaps disadvantaged. Or suffer from a new-found attention-deficiency syndrome. Mencken stated flatly that not all students belong in college.

Without doubt, Mencken today would not be free to write as he did. Indeed, the restrictive use of language is pervasive. Anthony Burgess observed that certain racist terms once regularly employed are taboo–"kike, sheeny, wog, wop and, most terrible of all, nigger." And the word "gay" has been reduced, Burgess wrote, to a "coy, giggly, totally inaccurate word." Similarly, many feminist scholars have called for the use of gender-neutral pronouns. Once acceptable terms are now clearly out of favor and, more important, self-censored for social conformity. Mencken is not singular. Shall we now delegate writers like Maugham, Conrad, Pound, Eliot, Belloc–or a composer like Wagner–to oblivion down an Orwellian "memory hole" for similar transgressions? That process is well underway and Mencken is one casualty.

Perhaps the most ignored of Mencken's traits is his unrelenting defense of individual freedom. His passion was free speech. It may be incongruous to modern readers that Mencken could defend that freedom with language that to contemporary sensibilities appears insulting. Mencken wrote with indignation of the denial by a Baltimore hotel to allow a black to speak. The poet Countee Cullen was ejected from the Baltimore City Club for attempting to give a talk. In the *Evening Sun*, Mencken fumed that "the rule forbidding coons to talk in the hotel is outrageous." The outrage in Baltimore then was not over the racial slur, but over the very idea that blacks should be allowed to speak in a public hotel. No one, including Mencken, even broached the thought that blacks might be allowed to register to stay in the hotel.

Nevertheless, Mencken fought for the freedoms that affected all. The famous Scopes trial, storied as a confrontation between Darwinian science and Christian fundamentalism, was to Mencken at bottom a conflict between government intrusion and speech. This clash of ideas and ideology was one of Mencken's finest hours. Similarly, the now-forgotten "Hatrack" episode in 1926 centered on free press and speech. The *American Mercury* came under attack from the Boston Watch and Ward Society, self-appointed guardians of public morality. The April issue, charged the Society, contained an excerpt, "Hatrack," from Herbert Asbury's *Up from Methodism* with "filthy, immoral and degrading" passages. The Society had suppressed the sale of some 75 books and sought to bar the *Mercury,* a magazine that had already mocked the efforts of Watch and Ward and ridiculed its leaders. Mencken sold a copy of his magazine in Boston Common. He was arrested, tried, and acquitted. Later he fought the Society and the Post Office department to retain mailing rights. Mencken's stand for press freedom was defiant and not without hazard. Several years later, Mencken again fought for, and won, freedom of expression and U. S. mail censorship when the Port of Philadelphia attempted to suppress the writings of Rabelais.

Mencken, the Baltimore newspaperman, battled for individual freedom to the end of his career. Almost a decade before Brown v. Board of Education, Mencken's last newspaper piece attacked segregation in the city's parks. Mencken, who personally felt all golfers were "idiots," argued that players should not be forced into separate-but-equal "distinctions and discriminations." Such practices, he wrote, "should not be imposed on free men in the Free State." Further, he observed: "It is high time that all such relics of Ku Klucery be wiped out in Maryland."

Unquestionably, Mencken was a bigot and prejudiced, with biased opinions of how people should comport themselves. He believed in the class system and the hierarchies of society. He believed in good breeding. Of course, he himself had no blue-blood pedigree and lacked many of the accoutrements of society. A *bourgeois* (perhaps the German term *burgher* is more appropriate), he displayed the Mencken coat of arms in his home–an ostentatious *gaucherie* that he would have mocked in others. But he also firmly believed in his right to write and say what he thought. He also argued forcefully for the right of others to say and write what they pleased, however preposterous. He deplored "quacks" but defended their right of expression. His views were unpopular seventy years ago and are less popular today. Most of all he mocked pomposity and disdained the fraudulent. "I don't give a damn," he once said, "what any American thinks of me." His manifold biases were non-partisan and his prejudices universal. Mencken's affirmation of the right to dissent is a continuing, if eroding, heritage in America. His bombast of stereotypes and name-calling remains the stock-in-trade of propagandists lacking HLM's eye-winking humor. Mencken remains a controversial figure who continues to confound friend and foe alike. Surely, the most interested observer of the continued contretemps is the shade of HLM himself, who loved nothing more than to "stir up the animals."

REFERENCES

Charles Angoff, *H. L. Mencken: A Portrait from Memory* (New York; Thomas Yoseloff, 1956).

Russell Baker, "Prejudices Without the Mask," *New York Times* [December 13, 1989] A31.

Anthony Burgess, *1985* (London: Arrow Books, 1978).

Malcolm Cowley, "Mencken and Mark Twain," *The Flower and the Leaf,* (New York: Penguin, 1985), 265-268.

Vincent Fitzpatrick, *H.L. Mencken* (New York: Unger/Continuum, 1989).

Anthony Julius, *T. S. Eliot, Anti-Semitism and Literary Form* (Cambridge: Cambridge University Press, 1996).

Edgar Kemler, *The Irreverent Mr. Mencken* (Boston: Little, Brown, 1950).

William L. Manchester, "Letters," *The New York Times Book Review* [February 4, 1990] 33.

_____, *Disturber of the Peace: The Life of H.L. Mencken,* 2d ed. (Amherst, Mass.: University of Massachusetts, 1986).

H.L. Mencken, *The Diary of H.L. Mencken,* Charles A. Fecher, ed. (New York: Knopf, 1989).

_____, *Prejudices: A Selection,* James T. Farrell, ed. (New York: Vintage, 1958/Baltimore: Johns Hopkins University Press, 1996).

_____, *The Impossible H.L. Mencken,* Marion Elizabeth Rodgers, ed. (New York: Anchor, 1991).

_____, *The Young Mencken: The Best of His Work,* Carl Bode, ed. (New York: Dial Press, 1973).

_____, *The Vintage Mencken,* Alistair Cooke, ed. (New York: Vintage, 1955/1990).

William Nolte, *H.L. Mencken: Literary Critic* (Middletown, Conn.: Wesleyan University Press, 1964).

Jonathan Yardley, "In Defense of Mencken," *The Miami Herald* [17 December 1989] N7.

Chapter Four

Talent Scout

H.L. MENCKEN SPENT CONSIDERABLE time and effort seeking out promising talent for his several enterprises. First and foremost, Mencken was a newspaperman, however, and he spent enormous time developing the potential in young writers. More specifically, he was always on the alert for talent, proved or prospective, that could make a contribution to the *Sunpapers*. His enterprise in this effort is described by Harold Williams in *The Baltimore Sun: 1837-1987,* which recounts some of his many expeditions into the South and far hinterlands with publisher Paul Patterson prospecting for writers of promise. Moreover, Mencken often sat in on the joint interviews held by the newspaper to sound out putative employees. Gerald W. Johnson was one of Mencken's prospects who proved to be a valued addition to the newspaper.

Mencken's literary discoveries, with co-editor George Jean Nathan, during his days on *The Smart Set* included the first American publication of James Joyce. The magazine provided an outlet for other foreign writers: Aldous Huxley, Joseph Conrad, and Somerset Maugham. Mencken introduced America to Bernard Shaw and Friedrich Nietzsche. Aspiring American writers found early acceptance in *The Smart Set*–S. N. Behrman, Damon Runyan, Sinclair Lewis, Edgar Lee Masters, John Gunther, Burton Rascoe, Thyra Sampter Winslow, James Branch Cabell, Ring Lardner, Maxwell Anderson, and Eugene O'Neill. Most became well-known and, for the most part, writers that Mencken praised and published are more apt to be remembered than those he dismissed. (However, he disliked some authors of considerable merit, among them Thomas Wolfe and Ernest Hemingway.)

Later, when Mencken became editor of the *American Mercury* his contacts helped him attract well-known literary figures such as Theodore Dreiser, F. Scott Fitzgerald, Sinclair Lewis, and Sherwood Anderson. He also published Margaret Mead, Emma Goldman, and Margaret Sanger. Unquestionably, Mencken an astute editor, knew talent when he saw it and his literary contributions are abundantly documented.

But in the 1920s Mencken turned up perhaps his greatest find that was not literary; a prize for the *Sunpapers,* an adornment for Baltimore, and a treasure for the nation. Edmund Duffy, a young and talented artist, came to HLM's attention in New York City and Mencken advised Patterson to take him on.

Duffy (1899-1962) was the editorial cartoonist for the *Sun,* the morning newspaper, from 1924 through 1948, three months shy of a quarter-century, and brought the newspaper three Pulitzer Prizes. Moreover, he was on personal terms with Mencken—information absent from most Mencken biographies, although Manchester's biography contains brief mention.

In 1924, Duffy was a staff cartoonist for the *Brooklyn Daily Eagle,* doing sports cartooning and sketches for the theatrical page of the stage and vaudeville personalities who played the borough. He also contributed reviews from time to time. Brooklyn, no longer an independent city after being annexed to New York in 1898, was a major theatrical center. The *Eagle* was a notable newspaper. Brooklyn's "Robbies" (not yet the Dodgers or "dem Bums"), was usually overmatched by Bill Terry's New York Giants; Duffy supplied his share of local sports cartoons, but he was a Giants fan. His greatest love, however was the theatrical crowd.

Duffy had little chance of breaking into editorial cartooning at the *Eagle,* where Nelson Harding had reigned since 1904, and was recognized as one of the best. (The only winner of consecutive Pulitzer Prizes, in 1927 and 1928.) Duffy had a brief career in editorial cartooning at the short-lived *New York Leader,* a worker-owned Socialist daily. Duffy's work for that forum was powerful, bold and emphatic in conveying its liberal message.

Duffy's cartoons, sober and somber, persuasive and leftist, reflected his training at the Art Students' League under the tutelage of John Sloan and Boardman Robinson.

Earlier, as Duffy later acknowledged, his "first job of any consequence" came with a series of drawings for the *New York Tribune,* for Armistice Day 1918. Credit for that assignment is usually attributed to Robert Benchley. Benchley and Duffy were good friends.

Nathaniel Benchley relates that Duffy, then with the *Eagle,* drew a cartoon of Benchley and his cronies–Dorothy Parker, George F. Kaufman, Robert Sherwood, F. P. Adams, and others–who lunched regularly at the Algonquin Hotel's Rose Room. Duffy's cartoon depicted the group as "the Round Table." No copy of this cartoon has been unearthed, but Benchley and others have affirmed it. The major point, however is that Benchley and Duffy were acquainted. Benchley was well known to Mencken, and they admired each other's work. Mencken was also acquainted with Boardman Robinson, a sometime *Sunpaper* contributor, an excellent artist whose Socialist, if not Communist, leanings precluded his full-time employment with the *Sun.* Robinson promoted Duffy, his former pupil.

The *Sunpaper* was in need of a full-time cartoonist, so the story goes, to help promote the newspaper's candidate for the 1924 presidential election, Democrat John W. Davis. At that time, the *Sun's* editorial page was occupied by J.N. "Ding" Darling, syndicated from the New York *Tribune.* Darling, immensely popular, but decidedly Republican, was cartoonist for the *Des Moines Register* and the *Sun,* seeking national stature through Mencken's recruits, required its own cartoonist. It is not inconceivable that HLM and Duffy met sometime during the long New York Democratic convention that landed Davis the nomination. In any event, Mencken convinced Patterson that Duffy would do and he came to the *Sun* in September 1924 on a 90-day trial. He stayed for a quarter-century.

Duffy's early efforts, frankly, paid little heed to Davis, the most conservative Democrat nominated in this century. But Duffy started flaying away at the Ku Klux Klan, Prohibition, and other ills that beset the republic. All were Mencken's favorite targets as well. The *Sun's* editorial pages took on a tone of seri-

Their Daily Bread

New York Leader, October 25, 1923

ous and sober cartoon messages that surely delighted Mencken. The editorial pages no longer bore a Republican slant that danced with the delightful frivolities of "Ding's" drawings.

When Mencken departed with a top team of *Sunpaper* reporters to cover the Scopes "Monkey Trial" in Dayton, Tenn., in July 1925, young Duffy came along to provide cartoons of the proceedings. The trial became a national sensation. The searing copy that Mencken submitted for that event should be studied today in journalism schools. Duffy did with his art what HLM did with his prose; it was a deadly one-two punch. Mencken, of course, filed his copy to the *Evening Sun;* Duffy's work was in the morning *Sun.* Baltimoreans were expected to subscribe to both papers. Both provoked outrage, locally as well as nationally. Mencken was already of national stature, but the exposure helped establish Duffy's reputation.

Nonetheless Mencken, as an advisor to Patterson, did not hesitate to suggest that the publisher direct Duffy to clean up his artwork and discard chalk for a crisp line: "he is young and ambitious and he will learn." This was presented to Patterson in one of HLM's periodic assaults on improving *Sunpaper* content, writing, and appearance. Mencken delighted in Duffy's art. A contemporary, John Stampone, then an admiring copy boy, relates that HLM would come into Duffy's office and chortle with glee amid much arm flapping over the offering being prepared for the next day's edition. Stampone, who went on to become a noted

---

Opposite: An early example of Edmund Duffy's editorial view, with a distinctly Socialist theme–the rampant inflation in post-war Germany. His style owes much to Boardman Robinson, his teacher at the Art Students' League. Duffy's artwork also compared favorably with the leading cartoonist of that era, Rollin Kirby of the New York World.

Maryland, My Maryland!

The Sun, December 6, 1931

editorial cartoonist himself for the *Army Times* in Washington, became a life-long friend of Duffy. Duffy and Mencken were friends socially as well as professionally.

After Mencken married Sara Powell Haardt, the two moved to quarters close to the Duffys; the wives, Anne Duffy and Sara, became close friends. Anne Duffy, an accomplished artist and decorator, helped Sara furnish the Menckens' apartments (and despaired at HLM's garish, if eclectic, taste). The Duffys' daughter, Sara Anne, was named after both women and is HLM's godchild. Anne was a daily visitor at Sara's hospital bedside during her final illness.

Duffy brought the *Sun* three Pulitzer Prizes–in 1931, 1933, and 1940, more than any other staffer in the newspaper's long history. In his way, Duffy brought notice and notoriety to Baltimore to match Mencken's. A *Sunpaper* colleague, Gerald W. Johnson, wrote that Duffy "was regarded with the uneasy delight that a zoo-keeper has in a particularly fine Bengal tiger... everybody shuddered to think what would happen if he ever went on a rampage."

Duffy went on a number of local rampages–one, in particular, against Maryland lynchings combined with his mentor Mencken, was sensational. On Maryland's Eastern Shore, a lynch mob pulled a confessed murderer from a local jail–a black who had murdered a popular local merchant–and Duffy's cartoon, "Maryland, My Maryland!" (opposite page) created a sen-

---

Opposite: The title is from Maryland's state anthem. Duffy's and Mencken's comment on a local lynching prompted riots and street demonstrations against the Sunpaper's *trucks. This was the kind of "rampage" that Gerald Johnson predicted Duffy would ignite.*

An Old Struggle Still Going On

The Sun, February 27, 1930

sation. The cartoon, combined with Mencken's searing commentary on the lawless citizenry, generated riots and demonstrations, and *Sunpaper* delivery trucks were overturned and burned; for the next twenty years, the *Sun* was anathema on Maryland's Eastern Shore.

Duffy attacked racetrack scandals and local political corruption as he skewered Teapot Dome, Coolidge, and Hoover–all Mencken targets. Duffy attacked the rise of Hitler and Nazism and noted the menace of Japan in the Pacific.

After a distinguished career, Duffy abruptly left the *Sun* in 1948, after his good friend and colleague Mencken had all but abandoned newspaper work. (HLM made his last great hurrah in the national political conventions for that year.) And several months later, Mencken himself was gone from newspapering. Mencken made incalculable contributions to the *Sunpapers* and helped create the respected institution it became. Mencken is rightly recognized for his notable contributions and discoveries in the literary world. Arguably the acquisition of Edmund Duffy, one of America's preeminent cartoonists, for his Baltimore newspaper must be accounted one of HLM's greatest discoveries of artistic talent.

Opposite: Mencken's selection of Edmund Duffy as the Sun's *editorial cartoonist paid off when Duffy was awarded that newspaper's first Pulitzer Prize, the first of three he was to win. The cartoon reflects Mencken's advice to clean up the drawings, not use messy chalk and to have a cleaner, bolder presentation. The subject was of Duffy's own choosing; Soviet Russia had not yet been recognized by the United States because of its "atheistic" ideology.*

REFERENCES ───────────────────────────────

Nathaniel Benchley, *Robert Benchley* (New York: McGraw-Hill, 1955).

S. L. Harrison, *The Editorial Art of Edmund Duffy* (Madison: Fairleigh Dickinson University Press, 1998).

_____, "'Wayward Press' Revisited: The Contributions of Robert Benchley," *Journalism History* (Spring 1993) 19-25.

Gerald W. Johnson, "Duffy, Stuffed Shirts' Foe," *New York Star* [24 June 1948] 28.

William L. Manchester, *The Sage of Baltimore: The Life and Riotous Times of H.L. Mencken* (London: Melrose, 1952).

Sara Mayfield, *The Constant Circle: H.L. Mencken and His Friends* (New York: Delacorte Press, 1968).

H.L. Mencken, *The New Mencken Letters,* Carl Bode, ed. (New York: Dial Press, 1977).

William Nolte, H.L. *Mencken: Literary Critic* (Middlesex, Conn.: Wesleyan University Press, 1964).

John Stampone, interview March 10, 1994.

Chapter Five

The Scopes Trial:
Mencken's Media Circus

THE ROARING TWENTIES, THE ERA OF Chicago gangsters, Prohibition, and bathtub gin are notable for their influence on American culture. Those kaleidoscope years left a legacy of sports icons–Bill Tilden, Babe Ruth and Bobby Jones; the musical genius George Gershwin and the romance of Jerome Kern's "Show Boat" as well as entertainment legends such as Al Jolson, Fanny Brice, and Will Rogers. Major social forces emerged–network radio, the vote for women and the rise of Wall Street–with significant repercussions. The 1920s were "an era of wonderful nonsense" with speakeasies, flappers and flag-pole sitters.

The Twenties witnessed an outpouring of national sentiment: adulation for aviation's "Lone Eagle," Charles Lindbergh; outrage over the unfolding scandals in President Warren G. Harding's administration; and the graft and corruption of Teapot Dome. Courtroom drama provided a common thread through those tumultuous years. Gaudy trials held Americans in rapt attention. The infamous Palmer raids, that netted 2,000 arrests in one day, and enforcement of the Volstead Act provided continuing fare. The conviction of anarchists Sacco and Vanzetti, victims of the big Red Scare, prompted protests in the streets. A nation first shocked by the horror of the Leopold-Loeb trial was later titillated by the Hall-Mills murder case.

Time romanticizes memories, however. The brutalities of Al Capone assume heroic proportions; people remember the daring of "Lucky Lindy" and forget the America Firster who openly backed the Nazi war machine. Similarly, one trial now enshrined in myth as a battle for religion was a great deal more. The theatrics of this event were captured in the 1945 play "Inherit the Wind" and a subsequent motion picture, dramas that helped perpetuate the prevailing myth of the Scopes trial.

In the mid-1920s one courtroom saga riveted the attention of the entire nation, the "Monkey Trial," (the derisive term was H.L. Mencken's), purportedly pitting the forces of Darwin's theory of evolution against the basic religious beliefs of Christian Fundamentalists. The defendant was John T. Scopes, a 24-year-old high school biology teacher. Actually, the Scopes trial was concocted by people who hoped to bring business and prosperity to a small town, aided by those who saw political opportunity beckon, and the event was manipulated by the press to capitalize on sensationalism.

The trial was dominated by a number of prominent figures who reduced Scopes to a minor role. Arguably, one of the most influential involved in that contest was H.L. Mencken, an eminent newspaperman and editor. Joseph Wood Krutch wrote, "the time will come when it will be generally recognized, as by a few it already is, that Mencken's was the best prose written in America during the twentieth century." Mencken managed to shape the Scopes trial in a manner that exceeds the role of a newsman reporting events.

When Mencken, nationally-known writer for the *Evening Sun* of Baltimore, led that newspaper's delegation to cover the Scopes trial in Dayton, Tennessee, in 1925, he spearheaded a distinguished group of reporters. The *Sunpapers'* staff was divided into two teams, from two competing but jointly-owned newspapers.

Mencken held forth on the editorial pages of the *Evening Sun,* with a regular Monday column. Another reporter from that paper was Henry M. Hyde, a member of the staff since 1920 after coming aboard from the *Chicago Tribune.* Frank R. Kent reported for the morning *Sun.* He later won national reputation and fame as author of *The Great Game of Politics* that became the title for his influential front-page political column, read for generations for its inside-Washington reporting, and J. Fred Essary.

Another member of that delegation, however, the youngest (only a year older than Scopes) and least-known, was the *Sun's* editorial-page cartoonist, Edmund Duffy. His graphic artwork played a significant role in the public's perception of the trial proceedings reported in the *Sun,* emerging as one of America's most influential newspapers.

For Duffy, it was his first out-of-town assignment and major news event since coming to Baltimore. Mencken, who loved nothing more than to "stir up the animals" saw promise in the Scopes trial that and more. In fact, the Scopes trial became a landmark episode in American journalism history.

The essential issue of the event, according to many, centered on First Amendment rights. Any threat to abridgement of speech and press was a life-long crusade with Mencken. In fact, Mencken had an ulterior motive: to humiliate William Jennings Bryan and, if possible, the entire state of Tennessee. The First Amendment was never threatened or challenged. Under the Constitution any state was free to dictate what is taught or not taught in its public schools. Mencken knew that, even if many of his newspaper colleagues appeared not to grasp that fundamental fact.

Duffy's contribution to the Scopes trial established him as a commanding editorial page presence. His art helped define the issues of the Scopes trial in graphic portrayal that complemented Mencken's scathing prose. Mencken put a lot of stock in a good newspaper cartoonist. "Give me a good editorial cartoonist," he reportedly said, "and I can fire half the editorial staff." The Scopes trial was largely a public relations event, engineered in large measure by Mencken himself.

In the mid-1920s a wave of anti-Darwinian sentiment arose, a belated reaction to decades of secular, anti-fundamentalist intellectual thought. Indignation swept across America's Southland–the "Bible belt" in Mencken's phrase. State after state passed resolutions prohibiting the teaching of evolution in the classroom. Florida, Kentucky, Texas, Arkansas and other states endorsed such measures. Tennessee was the first, however, to pass specific legislation in both houses and escape veto by the governor. Consequently, when the youthful Scopes freely admitted he taught evolution, he was charged with violating the new state law, a misdemeanor, and the battle was joined.

He Put Us On The Map

The Sun, May 25, 1925

From the outset the prosecution was amiable, if not friendly. Local people, seeking publicity for the obscure county seat of Dayton, sought to capitalize on the evolution issue. The trial was originally conceived as a kind of Chamber of Commerce spectacle to gain the town much-wanted publicity. Boosterism was a trait of the 1920s, dissected by Sinclair Lewis in his novel *Babbitt*. Informally, plans were hatched in a local drug-store over summer sodas and the amiable Scopes agreed to go along with the scheme to help put Dayton on the map. Dayton did, indeed, attract attention, but not in the manner anticipated.

Dayton boosters fought vigorously to keep the subsequent court action in town and away from nearby Chattanooga. Eventually, the publicity generated by the charges attracted the interest of the national American Civil Liberties Union (ACLU), who provided Scopes with the legal services of Dudley Field Malone and Arthur Garfield Hays, lawyers of national reputation. The impending clash came to Mencken's attention through his wide-spread clipping service and friends who alerted him to events unfolding in the obscure town in the Tennessee mountains. The Scopes trial began as a promotion, if not a circus. Circus tents and carnival hoop-la is precisely how Duffy portrayed it in an early editorial page cartoon, as he scoffed at the press agents and promoters of the event.

If the instigators of the prosecution of the willing Scopes envisioned nothing more than a civic promotion, others who became involved, including Mencken, viewed prospects more soberly. Scopes's first defense counsel, John Randolf Neal, a dis-

---

Opposite: As the Scopes trial approached Duffy began to portray the inhabitants of Dayton, Tennessee, as rubes and yokels. One of the goals of those who instigated the trial was to showcase Dayton and "put it on the map" commercially. Their efforts boomeranged.

A Closed Book In Tennessee

The Sun, June 19, 1925

tinguished former law school dean, put the issue succinctly: "The question...involves the freedom of teaching, or what is more important, the freedom of learning." On point of law, the dean was incorrect. He was replaced as senior defense counsel by others, however, who desired a broader fight.

William Jennings Bryan, for the prosecution, wanted to make battle against evolution for Fundamentalism. But the three-time Democratic presidential candidate and former Secretary of State under Woodrow Wilson, envisioned a broader agenda. The pious religious issue held high political potential. Bryan volunteered his services on behalf of the prosecution team and abandoned his thriving Coral Gables real estate promotions and public Sunday preaching in Miami to undertake the fight for the Lord in Dayton.

Bryan, apparently at the end of his political road, had made millions in real estate speculation and was adding to his wealth in Miami. But he craved political power. The Scopes crusade offered an opportunity to mount a powerful political machine fueled by a vast coalition of active Christians who might somehow vault Bryan back into a successful run for the presidency.

Mencken recognized the case for all these things, and saw the trial as another opportunity to denounce Bryan, as a fraud and a charlatan. The religious zealots could use this forum to right all that was wrong with teaching scientific thought and further repress disconcerting ideas in the classroom. Accordingly, Mencken personally convinced the famous criminal trial lawyer Clarence Darrow to defend Scopes. At bottom, Mencken sought to humiliate Bryan. "Nobody gives a damn about that yap school-

---

Opposite: Increasingly, Tennessee was portrayed as narrow and bigoted, and allowing only one book to be taught. In fact, every school district retains the Constitutional right to choose books and teachers, and the right to tell those teachers what to teach.

teacher. The thing to do is make a fool out of Bryan," he told Darrow, who agreed and took the case for the defense.

Darrow and Bryan were old adversaries who had clashed publicly over the Fundamentalist issue earlier in the pages of the *Chicago Tribune.* Bryan lost that skirmish. Through Mencken's connivance, the *Evening Sun,* arranged to put up the bond and pay any damages incurred by defendant Scopes. Clearly, Mencken's influence prompted the extensive role played by the *Sunpapers* in the Scopes trial. Mencken displayed deep interest in the failings of the South generally. His excoriation of the American South's supposed utter indifference to the arts, "The Sahara of the Bozart," had attracted national attention, and was a sore point in the South.

Events were clearly beyond Scopes himself as the trial grew in importance; he felt that things "got past control." Lawyers for each side, prominent and expensive, donated their services. Everyone recognized that Scopes was guilty, as charged, for violation of the Butler Law, as the legislation came to be known. Scopes himself freely admitted his violation. The case could have been disposed of in an afternoon. What the trial provided, however, was a public forum in open court before a jury for the issues to be debated. Darrow and Mencken looked beyond the inevitable conviction with relish to the follow-up appeal in a higher state court and perhaps eventually the Supreme Court of the United States. The fact that two titans of opposing thought would do battle publicly only served to stimulate interest.

As newspapers and leading magazines, like the liberal *Nation* and others took up the cause, the trial assumed national importance. As the ballyhoo mounted and visitors poured into town, events assumed the realization of a press agent's dream. Cartoonist Duffy presented the spectacle to his readers. Coverage of the trial itself in July 1925, as reported in the Baltimore newspapers, reflected in microcosm the several ways that the 50 to 200-plus (accounts vary) reporters and magazine writers covevolutionary and Fundamentalist views of man's origin assured almost universal interest. Mencken, the leading media celebrity, early identified the defendant as "the infidel Scopes" and the judicial process as the "Monkey trial" in Dayton, which he scoffingly described as "the new Jerusalem."

Local boosters saw their early hopes to attract favorable attention to Dayton begin to boomerang. News coverage was not complimentary. Mencken was simply being Mencken and his vitriolic copy that focused on the city, its inhabitants, and visitors was sought by newspapers across the country. The Chattanooga *News* ran his copy locally, sometimes expurgated.

The other members of the *Sunpapers'* team, Kent and Hyde, solid, sober newsmen, filed meticulous and objective stories. Duffy, sent back sketches of the townsfolk, the figures in the trial, and some of the jurors as they were selected. Duffy's renderings were not unkind, harsh caricatures. His artwork was stark and graphic, reflecting something of the raw-boned visage of the mountain people. Duffy's illustrations did not accompany the Mencken stories–more color pieces than news reporting–including HLM's classic portrait of the Klan and his night-time visitation to a revival meeting of Holy Rollers in the hills above Dayton.

Duffy's editorial art graced the solid news reporting of Frank Kent's dispatches for the *Sun*. Mencken provided readers of the *Evening Sun* with word pictures that placed them in the scene. Hyde wrote factual, straightforward accounts of the trial itself. But Mencken was not writing for Baltimore readers alone; many editors bought his work–the closest he ever came to news syndication in his career. Consequently, readers in Dayton saw his stories in the Chattanooga *News* and the contents inflamed the local citizenry who were justifiably angered at being described as "morons" and "yokels" and worse. The local papers cut much of this; Mencken complained that "the *News* makes a frightful hash of my stuff." Mencken was at the top of his form–slashing, scornful and vituperative–and his victims howled. He loved it.

Duffy made similar portrayals in his editorial cartoons. No humor lightened the scorn and contempt he felt for Bryan and his bigoted message. Subscribers in Baltimore were as upset as readers elsewhere. One official from the Baltimore Association of Commerce wrote to the editor of the *Sun,* complaining that the paper's "unjust characterization of the people in the South" had hurt the city's business with that part of the country. Duffy had to share that indictment; he was as adept at ridicule in his art as Mencken was with his prose. Each, in his own way,

Darrow Telling It To The Judge

The Sun, July 16, 1925

attacked Bryan and his ideas as the trial progressed.

Duffy and Mencken left Dayton before the trial was complete, however. Mencken's work was over, even if the trial was not. Even before he left Baltimore, Mencken's letters reveal that he had commitments to return to New York. His reporter's instinct did not desert him. The closing session was to be Darrow's summation and Mencken left the reporting to others. It was just as well Mencken left. Local ire was rising against him, as the exemplar of those who came to scoff and mock the proceedings. Mencken, apparently unaware of the genuine anger of the townspeople, narrowly escaped actual physical assault. The crowd had to be content with tearing him limb from limb in effigy. Kent and Hyde remained for the wrap-up of the trial.

Consequently, Mencken missed one of the greatest courtroom spectacles of the entire proceedings; the show-down performance with Darrow combating Bryan face to face. Darrow followed Mencken's early advice to make a fool of Bryan. He did. On the stand, Bryan defended his Fundamentalist beliefs as an expert witness. Evolution was no longer on trial; Bryan, self-appointed interpreter of God's word, became the defendant. Bryan's responses earned him widespread ridicule as he defended the literal meaning of the Holy Bible.

Publicly, it was the humiliating end of a once-great figure. Paradoxically, Bryan felt vindicated when defendant Scopes was convicted. Technically, the pious won; the law was later upheld by a Tennessee's higher court. Scopes's fine, however, was refund-

---

Opposite: This Duffy sketch (an excerpt from a front-page series of three) was made on the scene during the trial. Duffy was part of the Sunpaper *team headed by Mencken. Darrow for this occasion dressed the part for his appearance in the rural courthouse.*

A Courtroom Spectator

The Sun, July 18, 1925

ed on a technical ruling. The show was over.

Pitiably, Bryan himself failed to recognize the public's general perception and basked in triumph. He spoke of a national speaking tour and future political plans. Days after the trial he was dead, victim of a stroke brought on by a gargantuan Sunday dinner, combined with too many iced drinks and simmering summer heat. Mencken, in probably one of the few genuinely cruel acts of his public career, wrote a cutting editorial obituary for the *Evening Sun,* describing Bryan as "a charlatan, a mountebank, a zany without sense or dignity. A poor clod...." He later revised the first version into an even more savage lead editorial for the October issue of the *American Mercury.* The *Sunpapers,* in an effort to atone (and to meet the criticism), assigned Gerald W. Johnson the job of writing a more fitting elegy.

Duffy, Mencken's protege, did not deign to acknowledge Bryan's death. No cartoon of any kind appeared. No mention was noted of Bryan's worthy past as "the Great Commoner" and three-time Democratic presidential candidate, author of the famous "Cross of Gold" speech that inspired the Populist movement to seek political and economic reform. Duffy, a life-long liberal, was affronted by the religious bigotry he had seen espoused by a demagogue. Duffy, like most Irish Catholics, took his religion seriously. What he had witnessed in the American South was disturbing, and he was as unforgiving as Mencken.

Opposite: The spectators fascinated Duffy and he drew a number of portraits. Duffy's artwork appeared in the Sun, *usually on the front page, and accompanied Frank Kent's news dispatches. Mencken's reports of the Scopes trial appeared in the* Evening Sun.

Let There Be Darkness

The Sun, July 19, 1925

Later, Mencken privately said of Bryan and the Scopes episode, "Well, we killed the son of a bitch." Nevertheless, Mencken wrote to Sara Powell Haardt, that "Bryan's death fills me with sadness."

The forces of Fundamentalism fell back in brief disarray but the issue has never really disappeared. Campaigns against "Godless" teaching and book banning occur with relentless regularity to the present day. Dayton deservedly returned to obscurity, but still serves as a useful metaphor for concerned Americans to defend the right to speak and think. Mencken fought other battles for free speech, but to his dying day despaired over future prospects for that essential liberty.

REFERENCES ————————————————————————

Carl Bode, "Mencken, Darwin and God," *Mencken* (Baltimore: Johns Hopkins University Press, 1986), 264-278.

Edward Caudill, "The Roots of Bias: An Empiricist Press and Coverage of the Scopes Trial," *Journalism Monographs,* 114 (Columbia, S.C.: Association for Education in Journalism and Mass Communication, 1989).

Ray Ginger, *Six Days or Forever?: Tennessee v. John T. Scopes* (Boston: Beacon, 1958).

Margaret Case Harriman, *The Vicious Circle: The Story of the Algonquin Round Table* (New York: Rinehart, 1951).

Opposite: Although Duffy left before the trial was over, the outcome was in no doubt in anyone's mind: Scopes would be found guilty as charged.

Gerald W. Johnson, Frank R. Kent, H. L. Mencken and Hamilton Owens, *The Sunpapers of Baltimore: 1837-1937* (New York: Knopf, 1937).

Frank R. Kent, *The Great Game of Politics* (Garden City, N.Y.: Doubleday, 1923).

William L. Manchester, *The Sage of Baltimore: The Life and Riotous Times of H.L. Mencken* (London: Melrose, 1952).

H. L. Mencken, *The Impossible H.L. Mencken,* Marion Elizabeth Rodgers, ed. (New York: Anchor Books, 1991).

_____, *Newspaper Days: 1890-1936* (New York: Knopf, 1943/ Johns Hopkins University Press, 1996).

_____, *Thirty-five Years of Newspaper Work,* Fred Hobson, Vincent Fitzpatrick and Bradford Jacobs, eds. (Baltimore: Johns Hopkins University Press, 1994).

John T. Scopes and James Presley, *Center of the Storm: Memoirs of John T. Scopes,* (New York: Holt, 1967).

The Sun [Baltimore] and *The Evening Sun* [Baltimore], June-July 1925, *Sunpapers* Reference microfilms.

Harold A. Williams, *The Baltimore Sun: 1837-1987* (Baltimore: Johns Hopkins University Press, 1987).

Chapter Six

Mencken's War
Against the South

IN 1915 MENCKEN LOST HIS "FREE LANCE" column with the *Evening Sun* because of his vitriolic anti-British, pro-German commentary. Mencken's reputation began in Baltimore as an outspoken newspaper critic and he gained a national voice in 1908, when he was appointed Book Editor of the *Smart Set*. In 1914 he and George Jean Nathan became its co-editors.

Mencken's reputation grew through his literary and social commentary and his prose was provocative and sparkling. He was a battler against Puritanism, censorship, and sham. Mencken held a certain contempt, indeed, cynicism, toward American culture and his brilliant satire and boisterous prose attracted enthusiastic converts. Mencken brought, as Kazin wrote, "a new and uproarious gift for high comedy into a literature that had never been too quick to laugh." His *Smart Set* columns dealt with books and authors with a new violence of opinion and expression.

Before his *Evening Sun* column was curtailed during the war frenzy, Mencken focused his newspaper writing on attacking the buffoonery of society and exploring the American language. The move for reform that stimulated the Progressive Era saw little of his presence. The evils of modern society and economics went unexplored. The Muckrakers, so-named by Theodore Roosevelt for their inclination to see the sordidness of the American Dream, came and went with no help from Mencken. His participation was missing. Perhaps Mencken's innate cynicism prevented him from tilting at the windmill evils of big business that moved Ida Tarbell to explore the role of Standard Oil. The prevailing graft and corruption that roused Lincoln Steffens to report "the shame of the cities," found no help from Mencken. From time to time his newspaper columns would feint at the graft and corruption of municipal government. Graft and corruption there was aplenty, but unvexed by Mencken. The muckrakers found no help from him; he was no crusader. But the bleak cultural landscape he saw in America, particularly the South, roused his ire.

Barely fifty years after losing its war of independence and enduring an uneasy peace, the American South sustained another assault–this time an attack on its cultural and literary heritage. Eventually, the South regained its land and its government and The War was over, by no means forgiven or forgotten, but nonetheless over. The latter assault–similarly unforgiven–continues to rankle.

In 1917, Mencken, deprived of his *Evening Sun* pulpit, resorted to writing for the *New York Mail*. The *Mail* itself came under fire for its pro-German slant; it became one of forty-four newspapers shut down by the Wilson Administration's Sedition Act of 1918. Before that unhappy event, however, the *Mail* published Mencken's "The Sahara of the Bozart," in which he described the South as a cultural desert, bereft of artistic attainment and particularly destitute of literary achievement.

Mencken's article that first appeared in an obscure New York City newspaper 80 years ago, continues to engender defensive comment and–in certain Southern circles–creates as much controversy as the debate about Pickett's debacle at Gettysburg. Southern advocates continue to this day to assert the merits of their cause and to defend themselves and their region.

Hobson's *Serpent in Eden* deals with the issue in depth. He explains why did, or does anyone care about Mencken's opinion? The vast body of public opinion knows little and cares less about the controversy. But as Harvard College's A. Lawrence Lowell observed, "public opinion is the opinion of the public that counts." Mencken counted. More important, he influenced people who counted. Put simply, that is the reason why a significant segment of the literary South continues to repudiate Mencken.

To the modern generation, Mencken is virtually unknown and much of his work largely unread. Although often quoted, many people–and this includes academicians–remain unacquainted with Mencken's vast body of work. Not to put too fine a point upon it, Mencken is known largely by reputation rather than familiarity with his accomplishments or his writing.

Mencken demonstrated a gift for commentary that stimulated readers as he attacked with joyous and sometimes bombastic irreverence the standard American icons. His writing followed the principles of Bernard Shaw: the recognized orthodoxies provided the main targets. In his newspaper columns, initially, the church was ruled out of bounds, but when the clergy mounted attacks, his publisher yielded and Mencken's thrusts were unleashed against this inviting target as well. His prose was irreverent, audacious, and provocative, and he punctured any ripe topic with gusto and prose that sparkled.

Mencken was a productive writer; he recycled his work: first with his newspaper columns, then with his magazine articles, and then to a book. By 1903, he produced his first book, *Ventures Into Verse,* a collection of his poetry–that owed a great debt to Kipling–compiled from his newspaper writings. But Mencken was innovative as well. If not a creative thinker, Mencken was astute enough to recognize a good thing when he saw it. For example, he was the first in America, indeed, anywhere at all, to produce a critical collection of Bernard Shaw's plays. His *George Bernard Shaw: His Plays* [1905], provided an appreciation of the British author, a person much like Mencken himself: a journalist who thumbed his nose at moral conventions, dismissed Democracy as one of the worst forms of government, and made iconoclasm acceptable in polite society.

With his background in the German language, the result both of his own heritage and the rich amount of German language instruction in the Baltimore public schools when he was a boy, Mencken was able to undertake a translation of the writings of the philosopher Friedrich Nietzsche, despite holding a full-time newspaper job that demanded long and late hours. Mencken's *Philosophy of Friedrich Nietzsche* [1908] remains in print. A generous sampling of his early work can be found in Nolte's collection, *H.L. Mencken's Smart Set Criticism.*

Mencken, therefore, was a man on the move at thirty-seven, but not yet the renowned critic of national stature.

Mencken's polemic attacking the South (the deficiency of the beaux arts in the Old Confederacy) went practically unnoticed in its initial appearance. The nation was, after all, engaged in a noble war to end all war that occupied the mind of the nation. Nor was the *Mail* all that influential as a newspaper, tainted with accurate suspicion as notably pro-German. Moreover, Mencken had displayed a similar theme–anti-South, combined with anti-Puritanism and anti-British jabs in other articles. Mencken was primarily occupied with his anti-British theme during the war when he could get any of these articles published and he was usually not successful. Moreover, he was profoundly occupied with avoiding any form of military service and keeping himself out of harm's way as well. Mencken cannot be termed a draft-dodger, but it can be said that he took whatever steps were necessary to avoid conscription into wartime work. Mencken was also busy with other enterprises; his anti-South stance was not a crusade. Hectoring the Southland was merely another one of his periodic devices to "stir up the animals." Mencken turned his attention to books.

Working during the war years, Mencken produced two books in 1918, published by his advertising friend Philip Goodman, that yielded promising literary reviews but little in royalties: *Damn! A Book of Calumny* and *In Defense of Women*. But in the next year, under the publishing banner of Knopf, Mencken scored perhaps his greatest literary triumph with *The American Language*. The book was an instant success enthusiastically received by critics. Newspaper clips provided the research and stemmed from Mencken's continuing interest in language and, like most of his work, had its genesis in his newspaper articles and columns and a longer essay in the *Smart Set*. Bode calls it a "classic," without reservation. Mencken, the Baltimore newspaperman, attained literary rank and recognition on a lasting and national scale.

Mencken followed this success with another collection of his writings from the *Smart Set*, put into book form that was popular and well-received. The *Prejudices*, a collection of his best essays, became the first in a series that eventually ran to six volumes. (Farrell's collection, *Prejudices: A Selection,* gives readers opportunity to sample their flavor and includes "Sahara of the Bozart.") An expanded version of his *Evening Mail* article, "Sahara of the Bozart," appeared in the second volume of the series published in 1920, and it was this version of Mencken's commentary that captured nationwide attention.

In truth, initial reaction was not that notable; the counter-attack took some time to build. For example, Isaac Goldberg's 1925 biography, *The Man Mencken: A Biographical and Critical Biography*–one of the first to examine Mencken and his work–does not address the "Bozart" polemic. More than two decades later, Mencken himself included the essay in his personal collection of what he described as the "unobtainable writings" in the *Chrestomathy.* These were pieces that Mencken took especial care would not be neglected or forgotten.

In his opening paragraph, Mencken notes that in the "vast vacuity" of the American South "nearly the whole of Europe could be lost in that stupendous region and with room for the British Isles." Does geographic size make for a fertile ground of literary growth? Then China, Africa and perhaps India should have been candidates. No, this was merely more Mencken hyperbole. Yet, despite the South's vast size, Mencken laments, "it is almost as sterile, artistically, intellectually, culturally, as the Sahara Desert." Or, indeed, the Gobi Desert. That point is well taken, perhaps. But Mencken, a Victorian in the truest sense, was lamenting a "lost," perhaps mythical civilization that he sensed or wished once existed in America's ante-bellum South. Mencken's mind retained a vision of a noble land that never existed.

Clearly, he exaggerates the cultural measure of the Old South. Like Walter Scott's romantic notions of medieval knighthood, Mencken longed for a South that, in fact, never existed. What did exist had few notable cultural accomplishments. If that elegant civilization ever existed, it produced few major heroes, no cities of Grecian nobility or Roman splendor. The South in Mencken's mind was no more substantial than the ideals of Plato's lost Atlantis with its mythic glories. Mencken, in effect, castigated the South for failing to be what it never was.

No Southern city could ever hope to match the New England

civilization of a hundred years before, that could boast the literary heritage of the small village of Concord, Massachusetts, that
housed Emerson, Hawthorne, Thoreau, Channing, and Alcott at
one and the same time. But few in the North, West or East could,
for that matter. Mencken yearned for a South that never was
and contemplated a region bereft of all cultural values.

Mencken lamented the sparse talent to be found in all of the
once-proud Confederacy. Even the best, Virginia, the Old
Dominion,–"the most civilized of the Southern states, now as
always," with the exception of perhaps one individual,
Mencken's much-admired James Branch Cabell–lacked major
literary talent.

"You will not find a single Southern prose writer who can
actually write," Mencken noted. The worst state, Georgia–a
state that could boast of only a "fifth-rate" writer, Joel Chandler
Harris, was "more nearly representative of the region," wrote
Mencken in his dismissal. The first state was merely "senile,"
the second simply "crass," Mencken lamented as he described
the demise of a South that was once a "civilization of manifold
excellence...undoubtedly the best that these States have ever
seen." These words helped to inflame the vilification inflicted
on Mencken from all across the South.

Mencken endorsed the meretricious Cabell, but ignored
writers of merit–Virginia writers, no less. Ellen Glasgow, for
example (who was to win the Pulitzer Prize in 1942) had written
several works that signaled a literary champion. Her first, *The
Virginian,* described the South that Mencken mourned.
Similarly, Willa Cather, another Virginia native, had already
published work that was to outlast Cabell's; she won a Pulitzer in
1923. As a critic, Mencken clearly had his faults.

Mencken went beyond literary evaluation to exorcise all pre-
tensions of Southern culture. The South, he maintained, was not
only devoid of literary talent, but barren of

> ... critics, musical composers, painters, sculptors,
> architects...there is not even a bad one between
> the Potomac mud-flats and the Gulf. Not a historian.
> Not a theologian. Not a scientist. In all these fields

the South is an awe-inspiring blank–a brother
to Portugal, Serbia and Albania.

Modern readers, less familiar with Mencken's invective, may
be alarmed at the venom in his prose style. Mencken was neither
constructive nor kind in his criticism, and the result was venge-
ful and merciless response from an outraged region. *Serpent in
Eden* summarizes the attacks that came to Mencken, and those
attacks were augmented by Mencken's unparalleled assaults that
were to come in his newspaper articles that dealt specifically
with Tennessee and the spectacle of the Scopes "Monkey Trial"
in 1925 over Darwinian evolution theories. In Tennessee,
Mencken was dealing with religious bigotry and intolerance amid
a narrow-minded, provincial world. These subjects may even
today be dealt with in stinging prose, but Mencken was attacking
a culture and civilization idealized.

Mencken, as always, used hyperbole with bombastic zest and
a yeasty humor, ingredients that invariably offend. Surely, no
reader can be unaware that Mencken hoped to enrage. Clearly,
there was a kernel of truth in what he wrote, just as certainly,
with a bushel of buncombe thrown in to attract attention.

Perhaps in his role as magazine editor and critic, Mencken
was attempting to goad Southern writers into productivity on a
higher plane. As editor, Mencken certainly advanced and promoted the careers of a number of Southern writers–including
blacks and women–by publishing their work in the *Smart Set*
and later the *American Mercury*. Mencken was no do-gooder–he
lifelong thoroughly despised uplifters and their ilk, the "snooper"
determined to improve everyone else's morals–but he recognized
and encouraged good writing, whatever its source.

The South, as a region, was inhospitable to nourishing talent. But talent was there in plenty. A number of Southerners
roamed north and did well in letters and other arts, as Mencken
himself acknowledged. He and *Sunpaper* publisher Paul
Patterson made frequent trips to search out talent for the newspapers–and invariably travelled South.

Beyond the regional editorial and literary counter-attacks,
the Southern response to Mencken began with the emergence of
writers like William Faulkner and Thomas Wolfe. Mencken

remained tepid toward Faulkner–some stories were published in
the *American Mercury*–and ignored Faulkner's novels. The
record bears out the fact that Mencken could not abide Wolfe and
rejected every one of his offerings to the *Mercury*. Mencken
actually refused to read Wolfe's novels.

Initially, the out-pouring of vituperative denial, abuse and
howls of outrage did not surprise or even disturb Mencken; he
had, after all, thrown the bombshell and was delighted with the
response. He delightedly collected the abuse in his personal,
public scrapbook *Menckeniana: A Schimpflexicon* [1928]. What
astonished him, Gerald W. Johnson (a Southerner recruited by
Mencken to work on the *Sunpapers*) writes "was the counter-
storm of laughter and cheers that swept up from the same
region." Some of his victims welcomed the abuse.

"I know," Johnson notes, "that Mencken was dazed at first
and incredulous for some time." But with that realization,
Mencken also worked to create within the South an intellectual
climate that eventually became one of the most vigorous in the
nation.

The South listened to Mencken, took heed, rallied itself and
by mid-century had a proud roll-call of regional writers and literary work of quality. Much of that stimulus unquestionably
originated in response to Mencken. In later years, Mencken
modestly took partial credit for that revival–a renaissance that
led to regional literary excellence.

Mencken was too harsh on the American South; while he
lamented the passing of some Golden Age, he failed to credit the
region's accomplishments. For example, if the South no longer
produced poets, no region before or since produced a genius like
Edgar Allen Poe.

Poe died in Baltimore, Mencken's bastion, and it must be
remembered that Baltimore, well below the Mason-Dixon line, is
a city steeped in Southern tradition. Baltimore, if an atypical
Southern city, managed to produce a talented array of painters,
scientists, and academics of first rank in the nation–all of whom
were known to Mencken, but left off his list of Southern accomplishments.

Strangely enough, Mencken, a thoroughly political animal,
failed to cite the monumental accomplishments of Thomas

Jefferson, author of the Declaration of Independence and the founder of the University of Virginia. No one matched that contribution ever in the history of the Republic, from any region. Similarly, the contributors to American political theory, including Virginians George Mason and James Madison, were passed over. Madison surely should have been remembered as the major author of *The Federalist*, the greatest contribution to political theory to emerge from the American experience. To be sure, the South was not producing similar achievements, but neither was any other American region. The intellectual stature of Presidents (even Virginians like Woodrow Wilson), was abysmal; Mencken dismissed Wilson's public utterances and writing as "mush."

Perhaps the South that Mencken mourned was no more than a delusion, a self-indulgent myth that he himself created out of the turmoil of the war years. Perhaps the visceral reaction persisting against Mencken in portions of the South lacks foundation and is based on rancor. Nevertheless, his legacy is lasting. Perhaps the flowering of the South would have come about in time without Mencken's barbs. He certainly raised awareness and a challenge. The South owes a debt of gratitude to Mencken that remains an account outstanding.

REFERENCES ————————————————————————

Carl Bode, *Mencken* (Baltimore: Johns Hopkins University Press, 1986).

Isaac Goldberg, *The Man Mencken: A Biographical and Critical Biography* (New York: Simon and Schuster, 1925).

Fred C. Hobson, Jr. *Serpent in Eden: H.L. Mencken and the South* Gerald W. Johnson, Foreword (Chapel Hill: University of North Carolina Press, 1974).

Alfred Kazin, *On Native Grounds* 3rd ed. (New York: Harcourt Brace, 1982).

H.L. Mencken, *A Mencken Chrestomathy* (New York: knopf:1949/Vintage, 1982).

_____, *H.L. Mencken's Un-Neglected Anniversary*, P. J. Wingate, ed. (Hockesse, Del.: Holly Press, 1980).

_____, *Menckeniana: A Schimpflexikon.* H.L. Mencken, ed. (New York: Knopf, 1928).

_____, *Prefaces: A Selection.* James T. Farrell, ed. (Baltimore: Johns Hopkins University Press, 1996).

William A. Nolte, *H.L. Mencken: Literary Critic* (Middletown, Conn.: Wesleyan University Press, 1966).

Chapter Seven

Free Speech, Free Press

A NATION, THOMAS JEFFERSON OBSERVED, cannot be both ignorant and free. The Founding Fathers saw the circulation of
intelligence and opinion as a vital condition of democracy, more
specifically the need for a postal service regulated by the central
government was essential. This is one of the reasons that
Benjamin Franklin agreed to serve as the nation's first postmaster general and President George Washington appointed
Franklin to that position. Washington believed that newspapers,
the major source of opinion, albeit biased, politically partisan
and even radical, should have access to the mails. Hence, from
the outset of the Republic, government regulation of the mail
was recognized for its vital role in the dissemination of opinion,
with a grudging recognition that at times that opinion may be
fractious.

Government regulation can be used to impede that flow of
information when it is deemed in the best interests of the government to do so. During World War I, under the Espionage Act
of June 15, 1917, printed documents–newspapers–that would
tend, in the opinion of the government, to cause insubordination
dangerous to the pursuit of the war effort, were banned. Hence,
such information so determined by government officials under
the jurisdiction of the Executive Branch of government was
barred from traffic through the mails. Consequently, forty-four
newspapers and magazines were shut down under this law,
despite the First Amendment, simply because they decried the

government role in wartime activities. Thirty more newspapers and magazines were allowed to publish, provided war commentary was withheld.

H.L. Mencken, familiar with this kind of censorship, thoroughly deplored it and officials who invoked it. Mencken felt that freedom of expression, perhaps the most precious of liberties, was a tenuous right that had to be defended unremittingly "to the last limits of the endurable." Mencken's experience with the suppression of speech through government intervention and self-appointed censors of the morals and manners of Americans left him to the end of his life with a bitter outlook.

Mencken described himself as "an extreme libertarian"and placed only one limitation on free expression: "the point where free speech begins to collide with the right of privacy." No one has a right to be a nuisance to his neighbors. But the concept of free speech, despite the First Amendment, he felt was a myth: "The common notion that free speech prevails in the United States makes me laugh. It is actually hedged in enormously, both in peace and war." In his later years, Mencken commented: "Free speech is a very limited right in this country, as I have learned to my bitter experience, more than once."

Restriction of freedom of speech and press, despite Constitutional guarantees to the contrary, were a life-long antipathy of Mencken's. The Supreme Court has wrestled with these issues in, for example, the Schenk and Dennis cases. Mencken saw the issue straightforwardly under the Bill of Rights, where the First Amendment states unequivocally "Congress shall make no law..." that inhibits free speech or press. He would be classified as an "absolutist" today. That is, "no law" means no law. But censorship comes in many guises. Mencken had reason for his caustic view and his continuing crusade for free speech and press is generally neglected in most assessments of his work. Early in his career he made vigorous effort to see that Theodore Dreiser's controversial novel, *Sister Carrie,* was rescued from the oblivion of a publisher's warehouse and given the recognition that it deserved as a major contribution to American letters. For his efforts to defend the novel against charges of salacious immorality, Mencken won the admiration of Dreiser but encumbered himself with enemies, public and private.

His outspoken and popular "Free Lance" column, a weekly feature in the Baltimore *Evening Sun,* assaulted and enlightened readers with its attacks on orthodoxy and essays on the arts. It was blatantly elitist and appealed to an enlightened minority, "the civilized and intelligent people," Mencken noted. In contrast to "a plague of bad advisors of moral, political and economic charlatans," Mencken made point to note, who stand out from the "abnormally large proportion of ciphers–darkies, foreigners, invading yokels, professional loafers and so on." Mencken's own bias and German heritage assured that he would take up the side of Germany in any confrontation with Great Britain.

Inevitably, Mencken was forced to abandon his column with its outspoken German sympathies and anti-British sentiments by *Sunpapers'* management. Although he gave varying reasons from time to time–he was growing tired, other commitments interfered–it is clear that Mencken greatly resented this infringement of his rights, as he saw it. Publishers always have the right to restrict what their hired hands produce.

Censorship over pro-German sentiments increased in the nation. The Committee on Public Information, headed by George Creel, was formed to make a case for the Allied cause and to form public opinion awareness of any kind of disloyalty. The Espionage Act, for example, penalized any incitement to disloyalty or interference with recruiting and prohibited any false statement which might interfere with the prosecution of the war effort. More restrictive legislation followed with the Sedition Act of May 1918, which made punishable all statements that were scornful or strongly critical of the Constitution, the American form of government, the armed forces, the flag, or the military uniform. German-American publications, specifically, were subject to official censorship. Self-appointed patriots brought about the abolition of teaching German in the schools (Mencken had attended one such school). German Street in Baltimore, that bounded the *Sunpapers'* building, was renamed Redwood Street; cabbage became "liberty slaw," and some shopkeepers with German names were boycotted or burned out.

Always the company man, Mencken yielded his column gracefully in public: "I do not believe that mutiny on the quarterdeck should be tolerated." And so, his column ceased to exist in October 1915, but Mencken continued to express his pro-German stance in some of his editorial columns through 1916. After the war, Mencken deplored the arrests and prosecutions, the muzzling of non-conformist newspapers and magazines, and the propaganda of the Creel Commission itself. He further deplored "the tyrannies" of Wilson's government, the Post Office, and the Department of Justice. These were crimes, in Mencken's opinion, perpetrated by "blackmailers disguised as patriots, scoundrels aspiring to higher office, by weak, pusillanimous and dishonest judges, by hysterical juries and unconscionable newspapers."

If wartime hysteria and censorship silenced Mencken's criticism of the Wilson Administration and the politics of the time, he nevertheless, continued to fight censorship with his literary criticism. He defended Dreiser's *The Genius,* a work clearly inferior to *Sister Carrie* or even *The Financier,* against charges of immorality. Dreiser, in effect, was under attack, observed Mencken, for "the same muddled sense of Dreiser's essential hostility to all that is safe and regular...." Mencken initially urged Dreiser to pacify the censors by deleting some passages: "After all we are living in a country governed by Puritans and it is useless to beat them by frontal attack–at least at present," he wrote Dreiser.

The incident known as "Hatrack" came about through Mencken's *American Mercury* and its constant jibes and criticisms against the Puritan influence in American life. From its inception the magazine aroused rancor in the breasts of those who would protect the morals of unsuspecting, or even agreeable, readers. Censors–self-appointed or government appointed–determine what is best for all and particularly what is best for you. Mencken, Manchester notes, was personally anathema and a marked man to censors, especially because of his earlier defense of the Dreiser books.

In Boston, under the protection of the Watch and Ward Society, was a group that worked diligently to keep reading matter pure, led by the Rev. J. Frank Chase. Mencken and the *American Mercury* gave particular offense. In 1925, a piece ran in the *Mercury,* "Keeping the Puritans Pure," that infuriated Chase. Several months later, "Boston Twilight," a description of the decline of Boston culture by Charles Angoff, Mencken's assistant on the magazine, further aroused Chase. In April 1926, Angoff again mentioned Chase in a scornful article, "The Methodists."

That did it. Chase went to war and his god was Comstock, to protect the morals of America. To Mencken, he was a "pecksniff." Chase notified booksellers and the authorities that the April issue of the *Mercury* was "objectionable" because of an article titled "Hatrack," not the article attacking him. "Hatrack," written by Herbert Asbury, was excerpted from his book, *Up from Methodism.* Angoff, who grew to despise Mencken, recalls in his memoirs that it was he who saw merit in the article, not HLM. Mencken, in Angoff's version, was dubious: "A piece of rubbish." And it was Angoff who saw trouble ahead, not Mencken. When the United Press notified him of the Watch and Ward action, Manchester reports that Mencken described Chase as a "buffoon" and that the "wowsers" and "swine" in Boston never read the *Mercury* anyway. In his self-serving memoir, Angoff relates that it was he who went ahead on his own and remade the May issue to save trouble. Mencken documented the entire incident in ten volumes, deposited now with his other papers in the Enoch Pratt Free Library, in Baltimore.

Trouble came in form of a court fight, instigated by Mencken himself. Angoff, in his version, assures that Mencken, if given the choice, would not have printed "Hatrack" if he had known what was going to happen. "Hell, no...if you're going to fight the moralists, fight them with something that has high literary value in itself, that you're not ashamed of." Angoff recalls HLM saying: "Fighting for a principle with a piece of inferior goods is sheer foolishness." But fight Mencken did.

Mencken compiled his own copious history of the event and that saga is related in Bode's *The Editor, the Bluenose, and the Prostitute.* Unlike Angoff, Manchester and Bode give even, unbiased accounts of the episode.

As a matter of fact, Mencken knew from the beginnings of the *Mercury,* that with its unrelenting attack on Puritanism in America, the magazine was marked for eventual attack. As unflattering articles continued in the magazine, it was only a question of time. So the assault was not unexpected. Moreover,

In The Cradle Of Liberty

The Sun, April 7, 1926

Mencken knew that the charges would have to be fought rather than simply ignored, or worse would follow. Subsequently, Mencken met with his publisher, both Knopfs–father Samuel and son Alfred–and decided to engage Arthur Garfield Hays, one of the attorneys in the Scopes trial the year before who had made a favorable impression on Mencken with his assertive manner and bold style. Mencken and his attorneys met and Mencken was warned that he could, if he lost, be sentenced to prison for as much as two years.

"I'll go," Mencken said.

To force a court case, Mencken decided to go to Boston, sell a magazine to Chase and be arrested. The subsequent court case would test Chase and, hopefully, engender a great deal of free publicity. All of this was done. The press was notified; the wire associations and newspapers. Mencken wanted the publicity that he hoped to be favorable. Mencken, surrounded by the press, who presumably would be friendly, encountered Chase on Boston Common, took a silver half dollar–biting it, to prove its authenticity–and was arrested by Boston's vice squad. The reaction of the Boston press, with few exceptions, was less than friendly to Mencken's cause. Chase and the Watch and Ward enjoyed strong local support with strong political ties.

The trial was held next morning in Municipal Court before a magistrate, who it turned out, was impartial and fair in his rulings. He promised to read "Hatrack" overnight and return with a ruling. Mencken passed an uneasy night. He would not have been surprised if he had been convicted and sentenced. On April 2, he wrote Sara Powell Haardt "by the time you read this I may be in jail." He thought the charge "absurd" and threatened, if acquitted, "to start suit for damages against every direction" of the Boston Comstock Society. Nevertheless, he was worried.

Opposite: Boston's Watch and Ward Society attempted to ban sales of the American Mercury. *Edmund Duffy, in the* Baltimore Sun, *supported Mencken.*

On The "Hatrack"

The Sun, April 8, 1926

Moreover, the press reports were not nearly as friendly as Mencken had hoped. Most newspaper editors saw the event as a gaudy publicity stunt to promote the *Mercury* and sales of the magazine. This, in fact, was not the purpose. The April issue was sold out. Mencken adamantly refused to authorize another press run that could have been a bonanza, but Mencken did not wish to capitalize on this aspect.

After reading the "Hatrack" article, Judge James Parmenter ruled that "no offense had been committed" and ruled for a dismissal. Mencken was buoyed by the news and later that day lunched with students and professors at the Harvard Union and presented them with a handsome Maryland flag, "The Free State," that had been sent up from Baltimore by his *Sunpapers'* publisher.

"The battle was superb," Mencken wrote Sara Haardt, "and the victory was really riotous. The poor Comstocks are in full flight today." He announced that he was praying for "a permanent injunction against them [the Watch and Ward] and heavy damages." Celebrations and exaltations came to a close when Mencken learned from New York newspapers that the April issue of the *Mercury* had been barred from the mails.

Chase, after his setback in Boston, had gone to New York City to persuade the postmaster to ban the magazine. That issue was moot; the April issue had already been distributed. But Mencken recognized that if the next issue was similarly banned the magazine could be denied its second-class mailing privilege. No newspaper or magazine can exist economically if mailed at regular first-class postage rates.

For this reason, Mencken culled the lead article from the on-press May issue, "Sex and the Co-ed," and put a safe, bland piece in its place. Hays won an injunction against Chase and the

---

Opposite: With Mencken's acquittal, the snoopers–Mencken's word for self-appointed guardians of manners and morals– were sent packing.

Watch and Ward Society from further interfering with sales and distribution of the *Mercury.* In Washington, however, the Postmaster General balked at reversing the New York decision and a further injunction was won by Hays, but the Post Office appealed. In the end, the results were inconclusive. The injunction against the Watch and Ward held and kept that group at bay. Eventually, the Post Office was upheld. Mencken considered taking the case to the Supreme Court, but was dissuaded from further action by his legal counsel. The upshot was described by Mencken as "a Mexican stand-off."

Technically, the authorities won, but Mencken and the *Mercury* prevailed; it became the leading magazine voice and Mencken emerged as a symbol of freedom of speech. The battle cost the magazine some $20,000 in legal fees and uncounted loss from timid advertisers. Mencken's real loss and disappointment came from the one source where he had hoped for support.

He had looked for support from the newspapers. The trial was, after all, a defense of press and First Amendment freedoms. But the backing, what there was of it, was tepid at best. Mencken was generally disliked; most people are who are acerbic and outspoken. Therefore, the reaction was hostile; many newspapers saw the incident not as censorship, but as an advertising stunt. The *Journal* (Syracuse, N.Y.) called it "A Splendid Advertisement." Mencken was astonished that his motivations could be misconstrued. He had, after all, refrained from another press run that would have capitalized on the publicity.

But Mencken was not only personally disliked; many editors recalled his stance during the war and held him in low regard for that reason. A number of editors across the nation saw Mencken as a threat to the polity and sanctity of American ideas that were held dear. Mencken was an iconoclastic scoffer. The Boston *Herald* attacked Mencken as an "alien"and reminded readers of his Germanic preferences. Mencken viewed that newspaper as a "notable journalistic prostitute," so this reaction should have caused little surprise. But Mencken's reputation was damaged.

New York City newspapers were critical, for the most part. Two of the best, however, the *World* and the *Times,* gave friendly support. The *Herald Tribune* and the *Sun* were critical. The *Sun,* in a venomous vein, recalled Mencken's "Prussian influence." Elsewhere, Mencken was roundly lambasted by the Richmond *Times-Dispatch,* the Memphis *Commercial-Appeal* and his one-time booster, Josephus Daniels, described Mencken as an enemy of "the home, the church, the law, and order," in the Raleigh *News and Observer.* Even his own *Sunpapers* in Baltimore was divided. His home paper the *Evening Sun* gave support: the morning *Sun* deplored "Hatrack." Editorial cartoonist Edmund Duffy, never one to be swayed by editorial policy, lent his support.

Manchester reports that Mencken was bitter over the "almost universal reprobation" from newspapers, the group where he felt he should have received his greatest support. Undoubtedly, many editors and publishers saw Mencken's "Hatrack" episode as an opportunity to get even. The "accumulated animosities of years" were emptied, biographer Manchester writes.

The opposition had an unexpected effect: it encouraged even more and outrageous censorship in many areas across the country. Politicians, as they are apt to do so often, jumped on the burgeoning bandwagon. The move boomeranged. And the drawn out court decisions worked to Mencken's advantage. Chase died, as well. Mencken was unsurprised; his enemies had a way of disappearing suddenly, like Bryan after the Scopes trial.

In the end, Mencken benefited. The *Mercury* prospered and if the events failed to generate advertising, they served as good publicity vehicles, certainly for Mencken, his writing, and his reputation. The critic is never popular; the iconoclast never feted; the outspoken scoffer never welcome–especially when correct. But Americans to this day can call upon the arguments Mencken put forward in defense of the right to free speech and press. Mencken should be forever recognized for his unrelenting role as a defender of freedom of thought and ideas.

In his personal summing up, Mencken wrote: "To this day those who remember the case at all appear to believe that we won all along the line. Morally speaking, we undoubtedly did, but in the legal sense we were floored finally by three judges [in the Circuit Court]....It was an ending not without its ironies."

Mencken would be the first to applaud the right of editors to publish and readers to purchase whatever the marketplace sup-

ports. Unquestionably, however, Mencken would be the foremost critic to castigate the deplorable state to which much of
modern writing has descended. The "pornomaniacs" and
"quacks" that produced the pseudo-scientific "piffle" that
Mencken deplored owe much of their freedom to Mencken and
others like him. The growing ignorance that threatens democracy, as Thomas Jefferson warned, gains ground despite a broad-
ened freedom of expression.

Mencken, of course, to the end of his days despised
American democracy, thought most of its citizens morons, and
believed that many First Amendment freedoms were little more
than myth.

REFERENCES ──────────────────────────────

Charles Angoff, "The Hatrack Story," *H.L. Mencken: A Portrait
from Memory* (New York: Yoseloff, 1956), 40-53.

Carl Bode, "Mencken, Darwin, and God," *Mencken* (Baltimore:
Johns Hopkins University Press, 1988), 264-278.

William Manchester, "Banned in Boston," *The Sage of
Baltimore: The Life and Riotous Times of H. L. Mencken* (London:
Andrew Melrose, 1952), 157-173.

H.L. Mencken, *The Editor, the Bluenose, and the Prostitute,* Carl
Bode, ed. (Boulder, Col.: Roberts Rinehart, Inc., 1988).

Douglas C. Stenerson, *H.L. Mencken: Iconoclast from Baltimore*
(Chicago: University of Chicago Press, 1971).

Chapter Eight

Editorial
Guidelines

IN ADDITION TO A DISTINGUISHED CAREER as an exemplary author–more than thirty books in his lifetime–and well-nigh universal recognition as the foremost newspaperman of his generation, H. L. Mencken was also an editor of uncommon merit. Mencken's productive period encompasses such a vast sweep of time–over a half-century and much of that in the early years of the 1900s–that a great deal of his work is little known to most readers. Moreover, throughout his career Mencken tended to incorporate published materials into other work. The genesis of newspaper commentaries found their way into longer magazine articles, and eventually into a book. These pieces were also changed as they made their way into other books.

An excellent guide to this practice can be found in Schrader's *H. L. Mencken: A Descriptive Bibliography* (1998). Perhaps the best critical analysis of Mencken and his writing is Fecher's *Mencken: A Study of His Thought* (1978), especially the section "His Style." Fecher provides a fascinating guide for interested readers to track the meticulous care that Mencken put into his writing, his rewriting, and his several revisions. Writing was an unending process.

Mencken began his training in newspaper offices and people who did that sort of work–at least in that era–knew the power wielded by an editor's blue pencil. Copy was written out or typed (typewriters were rare in that era) in takes and then sent to be cast in hot type before a proof was pulled. Proofs were then read and more often than not, rewritten and corrected by a copy editor and a proof-reader, who did more than a read for grammar and syntax. A C.Q.—check this—meant that facts and spelling were thoroughly checked. Reporters merited a by-line only over a period of time, and then for better-than-average work.

Never in his career did Mencken question an editor's right to amend, rewrite, or alter his copy as submitted for just and correct reason. Mencken held to that credo. Nor did he, as editor, hesitate to change copy, rewrite copy, or make any textual changes thought to improve the printed product.

One of Mencken's early editorial adventures came in April 1912, when he and George Jean Nathan embarked on a new column, "Pertinent and Impertinent," for the *Smart Set*. The column was written in tandem under a pseudonym. Owen Hatteras was the name selected; Owen replaced John, an earlier version, because as Nathan explained "it sounded more capricious." Mencken wrote under a number of names for the *Smart Set*–Herbert Winslow Archer, C. Farley Anderson, Pierre d'Aubigy, William Drayham, William Fink, Amelia Hatteras, Harriet Morgan, George Weems Peregoy, James P. Ratcliff, Ph.D., and Watson and Woodruff. Mencken employed numerous other pseudonyms in other publications. Without question, however, Owen Hatteras was his finest creation.

Major Owen Arthur James Hatteras, D. S. O., returned from WW I a decorated hero, and acquired a life of his own. His was a brief existence, barely more than a dozen years, but he managed to express the opinions of his creators in his column. Nathan, with drama and the theater, but mostly Mencken with his attacks on marriage, romantic love, and sentimentality. Hatteras, like his creators, jeered at reformers, preachers, politicians, and professors. Boors, bores, and boosters provided continuous targets. Hatteras occasionally appeared in a feature article, often to the consternation of the original writers who had submitted the piece. Presumably, Hatteras "died" when his creators went over to the *American Mercury;* his obituary was noted in several newspapers. Hatteras later showed up in Mencken's collection *A New Dictionary of Quotations* (1942); Mencken's subtle sense of humor was often unobserved.

In one of Hatteras' greatest contributions, the "Americas"

column, Mencken was able to print without comment representative newspaper stories which illustrated the insipid idiocy of
what passed for ideas and thought around the nation: florid boosterism from the mid-West; blessings on the Ku Klux Klan from
West Virginia, plus the usual Mencken targets–anti-Darwinism,
Fundamentalism, and Prohibition.

Mencken and Nathan operated under a simple fundamental
rule: one veto would kill a proposed article. Each Monday,
Mencken would pick up his bundle of manuscripts from the
Central Post Office in Baltimore and read through each of the
offerings. Those that passed went to Nathan in New York.
Manuscripts rejected by Nathan were returned with a rejection
notice, short and to the point; these notes would give some
advice on what was wrong and why, or offer encouragement.

As editor, Mencken followed a basic rule that Nathan
endorsed: when in the office, neither would speak until 11:00
a.m., not to each other or anyone else. In a June 1921 column,
edited by Hatteras, that purported to be a conversation between
Nathan and Mencken, Mencken presented his views "On Editing
a Magazine":

> The magazine editor is simply a scoundrel. In
> his dealings with authors he is utterly without
> conscience....His one aim is to sell his puerile
> and scabrous magazine. If he can do by debauch-
> ing and degrading an author, he never hesitates an
> instant. The beaches of beautiful letters are covered
> with his victims.... No one can pass through
> the magazines without gross damage to his
> spiritual kidneys. For this the editor is to blame.

Any author today can endorse these sentiments. Mencken,
the author, surely agreed with the strong feelings expressed by
Hatteras, that is, Mencken the editor.

As a critic, Mencken helped to introduce a generation of
American readers to writers of promise and did not hesitate to
beat the drum for those unknowns who came to contribute a
great deal to the literary scene. Nor did he lack the gusto to dis-
miss as "piffle" the authors who were acclaimed by others. In an

article in the *Smart Set* of November 1920, Mencken reported the results of his offer to writers of neglected manuscripts to send them to him. "A tidal wave of manuscripts gushed upon me from all parts of the country," he wrote, "and I was weeks working my way through them."

Of the entire lot, Mencken said, only one showed promise and this by an author once published. The ms was duly sent along by Mencken to a publisher who accepted and published the work. Not a single manuscript that came his way was, in his opinion, worthy of further reading. Moreover, Mencken reports, "a good many sent me abusive letters after I had returned their manuscripts, but only one thanked me for my exertions."

Mencken fostered the career of several writers–James Branch Cabell, F. Scott Fitzgerald, Ben Hecht, Sherwood Anderson, Dashiell Hammet, Willa Cather, Ruth Suckow, Elizabeth Saxway Holding, and Floyd Dell, for example, and continued to promote those published authors whose prospects needed support–Theodore Dreiser, Sinclair Lewis, and Joseph Conrad. The cardinal rule of Mencken and Nathan's *Smart Set* policy was to discover new American authors and to give them opportunity to reach an intelligent and sophisticated audience. Through its pages, the magazine introduced the early work of Eugene O'Neill, Zoe Atkins, and Rita Wellman.

Other editorial rules were:

"To present the point of view of the civilized minority; to introduce the best foreign writers to America." Some of these included Lord Dunsany, James Joyce, Somerset Maugham, Aldous Huxley, Harold Brighouse, and Phyllis Bottome.

Further *Smart Set* goals were "to leaven the national literature with wit and humor" and to encourage sound poetry. The latter goal perhaps left something to be desired, but included the work of John McClure and John V. A. Weaver. And every eight or ten months, Mencken gave over his review column to a roundup of books of verse. Ezra Pound fared well, as did Amy Lowell, but Harriet Monroe and others were less well received.

If editing was a thankless job intellectually, it proved to be highly remunerative and Mencken nevertheless enjoyed it; indeed, rejoiced in the effort and never neglected his duties. But a misstep as editor led to Mencken's leaving the *Smart Set*.

Circulation was declining and the magazine faced growing competition, but Mencken's satiric comment on President Harding's funeral train in the September 1923 issue hastened his departure. Mencken saw no reason to pull his punches on the hapless Harding, whom he had regularly roasted during his inept and corrupt administration. The article offended the publisher, however, who ordered the piece pulled and announced plans to sell the magazine.

This marked the end of Mencken's reign at the *Smart Set* and opened the way for him to begin the *American Mercury,* under Alfred Knopf's ownership. Nathan also came along, but the enterprise was clearly Mencken's. The inaugural issue was January 1924. "The aim of the the *American Mercury* will be to offer a comprehensive picture critically presented," stated the prospectus, "of the entire American scene."

Mencken continued to develop and encourage new writers. Moreover, he brought black writers to the fore: W.E.B. DuBois, Countee Cullen, James Welden Johnson, and Langston Hughes. And as C. Vann Woodward notes, the black writer George S. Schuyler "appeared more frequently in the magazine's final years under Mencken's editorship than any writer of any race." But Mencken also opened up the pages of the *Mercury* to articles on medicine, science and social thought and brought many of these authors to prominence: Raymond Pearl, Paul de Kruif, and Logan Clendening. Mencken seldom accepted an article that he did not agree with and worked closely with authors from early draft to final galley pages, even though some chaffed at Mencken's liberal sprinkling of honorifics–Hon. and Dr.–that he so loved and included lavishly in his own writings.

Throughout his career at the *Mercury,* Mencken attempted to get the best writers on any subject; if he could not get the best writer, he would persuade the best scientist to tell the best story and he saw that it was well written. Usually, Mencken sought out the writers he wanted for the subjects he desired, but he welcomed work from any who wished to apply. The writers who sought to break into the *Mercury* were given direction by *Writer's Market* and the editor Aaron M. Mathieu warned prospective writers that the magazine sought "strongly opinionated" contributions. In the 1930 edition, Mencken spelled out

The Evening Sun, April 9, 1938

the guidelines, aimed at the putative writer-contributor seeking an outlet for literary production.:

> The *American Mercury* does not neglect *belles lettres*, but it makes no apology for devoting little space to mere writing. Its fundamental purpose is to depict and interpret the America that is in being; not the America that might be or ought to be. It would print more short stories if more good ones could be found.

Until his departure with the December 1933 issue, Mencken created in the *Mercury* perhaps the preeminent magazine of American letters. But by the onset of the Great Depression, its pages lost some of that early incandescence. Its influence and effectiveness waned because of the changing economic conditions, and no one, not even Mencken, could maintain the pace of editorial innovation that he brought to the *Mercury*. But while it lasted, throughout his tenure as editor, the *Mercury* was glorious adventure and few magazines have approached its influence.

Mencken paid particular editorial attention to an English teacher at Baltimore's Goucher College, Sara Powell Haardt. She managed to be published in the *Smart Set* and undertook the chores associated with Mencken's compilation of abuse directed toward him in *Menckeniana: A Schimpflexikon* (1928). Haardt, whom Mencken married in 1930, was a writer of some substance, who managed to be published in the *American Mercury* as well as a number of other magazines, some literary and some so-called women's magazines. Haardt also went to Hollywood as a screenwriter for Famous Players-Lasky-Paramount Studios and Mencken followed her career with editorial assistance in all

---

Opposite: Editor Mencken was innovative in his use of graphics during his reign as editor of the Evening Sun's *editorial page. Here he devotes the entire page width for an Edmund Duffy cartoon to deliver a blistering attack on President Franklin D. Roosevelt's New Deal relief policies. Mencken thoroughly detested Roosevelt.*

The Evening Sun, February 10, 1938

of her work. She did well on her own, but Mencken was fully involved and sought unsuccessfully to inveigle her into writing a screen treatment of Swift's *Gulliver's Travels.* She was a frequent contributor to the pages of the *Sunpapers,* where Mencken was not without influence. Her published work is clearly stamped with Mencken's Teutonic interjections that he so loved, and the honorific Drs. he scattered through his own text. Haardt yielded, unlike other writers; Arthur Krock, for instance, who simply struck out the Mencken additions.

Mencken's last editing for Haardt was after her death; Mencken gathered a collection of her stories and added a preface both instructive and insightful. The finished volume, *Southern Album,* was sent by Mencken with his personal card to universities and colleges in America. It was a labor of love.

Mencken was a good editor, but an obtrusive one. Through the 1920s and 1930s Mencken supplied a continuing flow of notes and comments to publisher Paul Patterson pertaining to the appearance and content of the *Sunpapers.* During one period in 1938, when he was assigned editorship of the *Evening Sun's* editorial page, Mencken wrote most of the editorials single handedly and simply threw out those written by those with whom he disagreed. Mencken's innovative graphics produced notable contributions—the splash of full-page width cartoons by Edmund Duffy and the Benday-dotted page of government employees. Sadly, as a newspaper editor, Mencken could not delegate; as an editor, he was an autocrat.

His last chores as editor, during the late 1930s and early 1940s, were given over to his personal papers, a massive enterprise that comprised setting the record straight for material that

---

Opposite: Mencken was daring in his use of the editorial page. He used an entire page with one column of text to create a stark illustrative editorial showing, with 1,000,750 Benday dots (reproduced here with a screen) the number of Federal jobholders, a deplorable number by Mencken's reckoning. Today, Civil Service jobs total 1.9 million; 4.25 million including postal and military jobs.

would not appear for years after his death. For his diary, Mencken amassed 2,100 pages and more than half of those remain unpublished. For his reminiscences as author and editor, Mencken prepared some 1,732 pages, of which less than half have been published. For his newspaper recollections, most of which center on the *Sunpapers,* Mencken compiled 2,748 pages and more than half of this commentary remains unpublished. Clearly, a good deal of the unpublished portions will remain so because they are repetitive, deal with arcane and forgotten subjects and people best left undisturbed

Mencken's works, and those authors that he guided into print, remain a legacy of American letters likely to be unmatched for literary quality for the twentieth century.

REFERENCES

Stephen Barr, "A Much Bigger Work Force," *The Washington Post* [December 28, 1998] A23.

Charles Fecher, *Mencken: A Study of His Thought* (New York: Knopf, 1998).

H. L. Mencken, *H.L. Mencken's Smart Set Criticism,* 2d ed., William H. Nolte, ed. (Washington: Regnery Gateway Editions, 1987).

_____, *Mencken and Sara: A Life in Letters,* Marion Elizabeth Rodgers, ed. (New York: Anchor/Doubleday, 1987).

_____, *My Life as Author and Editor,* Jonathan Yardley, ed. (New York: Vintage/Random House, 1995).

Richard Schrader, *H.L. Mencken: A Descriptive Bibliography* (Pittsburgh: University of Pittsburgh Press, 1998).

C. Vann Woodward, "Baltimore's Mencken," *Menckeniana* 136 (Winter 1995) 1-6.

The Writer's Market, Aron M. Mathieu, ed. (New York: Writer's Digest, 1930).

Chapter Nine

Schimpflexikon Updated

IN 1928, WITH THE EDITORIAL ASSISTANCE OF Sara Powell Haardt, H. L. Mencken happily published a 132-page collection of invective, character assassinations, and related insults directed at him. These he had lovingly gathered over a number of years, at considerable personal cost for the national clipping service that searched out any comments in print.

The result was *Menckeniana: A Schimpflexikon,* a book titled with another of those arcane Teutonic constructions that Mencken delighted in employing to enrich the lexicon and confound and impress readers.

Under twenty-three separate headings, beginning with Zoological (headings were not arranged alphabetically), Mencken gathered epithets from a variety of sources- newspapers, books, magazines, and radio broadcasts–in no particular order, chronological or otherwise. From the first entry "... he is a weasel," to the last, "A Baltimore Babbitt," (from O.O. McIntyre, a one-time popular columnist), the 422 entries–from no more than one word to a page-and-a-half–were chosen, Mencken tells us, "for their wit–for there are palpable hits among them!"–for their "blistering ferocity," and others for their "charming idiocy."

Like the original, this collection is "not exhaustive." But an effort has been made to keep entries, like the original, "representative." Today there are far fewer from which to choose. In 1926 alone, more than 500 newspaper editorials commented on

Mencken; modern observers do not devote nearly as much attention to Mencken, but he has been dead for forty years. Unquestionably, Mencken retains the power to offend and outrage large numbers of people, many of whom rarely read what he wrote. Most readers to this day, in fact, remain blithely unaware that Mencken was a monumental humorist albeit of the blackest kind. His sardonic japes today would escape most of his targets, as in an earlier era many went unrecognized.

He continues to be denounced vigorously and occasionally at length. Surely, Mencken would be among the first to applaud any effort to provide an appendage of modern specimens of brickbats sent his way. One of Mencken's greatest delights was to "stir up the animals" and the animals continue to be restless.

ANTI-SEMITISM

"Let it be said at once, clearly and unequivocally: Mencken was an anti-Semite."
Charles A. Fecher, Introduction,
The Diary of H. L. Mencken, 1989

HEALTH

[On his *Diary*] "...it is an exercise in hypochondria..."
New York Review of Books, 1990

ELITISM

"...world-class literary gourmand..."
City Paper [Wash., D.C.], 1992

"Mencken celebrated elitism before the term was invented."
Los Angeles Times, 1993

CHARACTER TRAITS

"Mencken would not forgive or forget–if there was anything to forgive or forget."
Charles Angoff,
HLM: Portrait from Memory

"In his stubborn conservatism and conscienceless jubilations, he was–dare we say it?–a yokel."
John Updike, *The New Yorker*, 1992

"Mencken tilts at windmills, in Baltimore and points far beyond, with gusto..."
Jonathan Yardley, *The Washington Post*, 1994

"...abrasive, self-confident and self-contradictory..."
Terry Teachout, *New York Times Book Review*, 1993

"...vivid, fanged, offensive all at once."
Los Angeles Times, 1993

"...an aberrant anachronism..."
Journal of American Culture, 1992

"...an ancient misanthrope..."
Wilmington [N.C.] *Evening Star*, 1993

"...a petty and mean-spirited man..."
Los Angeles Times, 1993

WRITINGS

"All his life, Mencken apparently yearned to be known as something more than a journalist–as a man of great learning."
Charles Angoff,
HLM: Portrait from Memory

"Here [*Minority Report*] you have to take account inescapably of his habitual confusion and his dogmatic German brutality."

Edmund Wilson, *The New Yorker*, 1969

"...crusty, curmudgeonly..."

Chicago Tribune, 1992

"...a formidable cynic..."

San Francisco *Sun-Reporter*, 1993

"...cynics like H. L. Mencken..."

Huntsville, Ala. *News*, 1993

Tim Giago rejected the H.L. Mencken Writing Award "after finding out the extent of Mencken's racism" [Giago prudently kept the prize money, however].

Billings (Mont.) *Gazette*, 1993

TABLE HABITS

His table manners are based upon provincial French principles, with modifications suggested by the Cossacks of the Don.

George Jean Nathan, *Pistols for Two*

WOMEN

"Women, according to Mencken, had intelligence only for one thing, to snare a husband or lover, and to keep him snared. To impute any other form of intelligence to women, he claimed, was to be sentimental."

Charles Angoff,
HLM: Portrait from Memory

Chapter Ten

Marching into
the Millennium

DEAD FOR MORE THAN FORTY YEARS, H.L. Mencken, who last wrote for a daily newspaper a half-century ago, shows no signs of fading into oblivion. From his newspaper beginnings in the 1890s, Mencken's literary presence promises to carry into the millennium and the twenty-first century.

Since 1989, five major books of Henry Louis Mencken's writings have been published, to be added to the 30-odd produced in his lifetime. A collection of his newspaper stories was published in 1991. In 1994, a major biography appeared; more than a dozen books dealing with his life and works have been published, the first in 1925. Two more biographies are in preparation. A collection of his writings, many in book form for the first time, *A Second Mencken Chrestomathy,* was published in 1995. Mencken's first gathering of his "unobtainable writings," *Chrestomathy* [1949], was reissued in 1982 and remains in print. Interest was stimulated with the unsealing of Mencken's papers by his literary executor, the Enoch Pratt Free Library, repository of most of his documents. Throughout his life, HLM supplied hundreds of blue buckram volumes along with diaries and papers stipulating delayed access and publication. Other Mencken holdings are at the New York Public Library, Yale, Princeton, and Harvard Universities and Dartmouth College as well as some thirty other colleges and libraries.

Several bibliographies identify Mencken's work: Betty Adler, *H.L.M.: The Mencken Bibliography* [1961], was for many years the standard. The newest, Richard Schrader, *H.L. Mencken: A Descriptive Bibliography* [1998] contains a chronology and descriptive analysis. The discussion here provides a broad overview of Mencken's work and noteworthy books dealing with the man, his work, and his influence.

The first major work published from Mencken's private papers was the *Diary of H. L. Mencken* [1989], edited by Charles A. Fecher. Some 1,400 pages (only one-third of the original contents) were published. The diary revealed Mencken's hitherto private opinions and provoked controversy with the flat charge by Fecher that Mencken was "clearly and unequivocally" an anti Semite. Mencken, always outspoken in his public writings, became newsworthy to a new and more-sensitive generation unfamiliar with his scathing style. Mencken dead created controversy as he had in life.

For example, the National Press Club removed Mencken's name from its library (a reaction that would have delighted him). The charges of anti-Semitism distressed admirers of Mencken and a number with impressive literary credentials refuted the charges, including Russell Baker, Jonathan Yardley, and William Manchester. Mencken is anti-Semitic, judged by modern correctness. In his time, perhaps not. The essential point, however, was that people were talking about Mencken and that would have pleased him immensely.

The renewed interest led to publication of a collection of Mencken's best newspaper work, spanning a half-century [1991]. Many of those pieces introduced a new generation to Mencken's scathing indictment of politicians, poltroons, charlatans, and frauds whom HLM robustly condemned.

Additional material focusing on his magazine career was published in 1993, with Mencken's private commentary on *My Life as Author and Editor.* That material revealed Mencken's less-than-flattering assessment of some of his colleagues and confirmed suspicions that Mencken was anti-Semitic, at least in his private thoughts. The first biography to benefit from the long-embargoed Mencken papers was Hobson's *Mencken: A Life* [1994], confirming with additional detail than Bode's *Mencken* [1973] that Mencken was less than a gentleman in many of his relations with women. By today's standards, HLM was a thorough-going womanizer, not above seducing aspiring writers into his bed, if not into his magazine.

The final trove of private papers, dealing with Mencken's newspaper recollections, *Thirty-five Years of Newspaper Work* [1994], revealed that Mencken also had some harsh private thoughts regarding some *Sunpaper* colleagues, a number of whom counted themselves friends.

Mencken's journalistic contributions, his critical writing, and his seminal influence on letters is enthusiastically recognized by literary historians and scholars but generally neglected in journalism classrooms. He was a major national figure through mid-century: newspaperman, primarily with the Baltimore *Sunpapers;* magazine editor (the *Smart Set* and the *American Mercury*); literary critic, political commentator and humorist; philologist (*The American Language*); and author of more than thirty books.

Despite his stature as a newspaperman–and he was, Louis Rubin notes, "the very best in the business"–Mencken is little known to journalism students. His literary influence in twentieth century America, vouchsafed by critics like Edmund Wilson, Walter Lippmann, Joseph Wood Krutch and Alfred Kazin, is duly noted in college literature seminars. Perhaps Mencken's absence in journalism classrooms, despite interest elsewhere, may be explained by the fact that his newspaper career flowered before the first World War, then reemerged only to disappear by the onset of the Great Depression. The answer may be that the journalist-academicians reject Mencken out of long-standing rancor. Mencken, an unparalleled iconoclast constantly embroiled in controversy, took a dim view of American journalism generally. He routinely described journalism academics as "fifth rate," or who were either "decayed editorial writers" or "unsuccessful reporters." Schools of journalism he held in equally low regard:

On the one hand, they are seldom manned
by men of any genuine professional standing,
or of any firm notion of what journalism is about.
On the other hand, they are nearly all too easy in
their requirements for admission. Probably half of
them, indeed, are simply refuges for students too

> stupid to tackle the other professions. They
> offer snap courses, and they promise quick
> jobs. The result is that the graduates coming
> out of them are mainly second-raters–that
> young men and women issuing from the
> general arts courses make better journalistic
> material.

If any of these observations remain valid (some certainly are), little likelihood exists that these failings will be rectified in today's classrooms.   Mencken was a debunker who battled against mediocrity. He vigorously attacked sham, pretension, hypocrisy, Fundamentalists, and Puritanism–taboo topics still on many modern college campuses. A number of the nation's states regularly exercise their Constitutional authority to ban books and topics deemed unsuitable for the classroom. Mencken's defense of First Amendment freedoms is often interpreted as attacks on religion–all controversial topics best avoided in today's politically-sensitive classrooms.

Nevertheless, Mencken continues to enchant a significant audience. A number of Mencken's contemporaries rate a footnote in journalism history or a biography or two, but few of the newspaper giants of his day–Herbert Bayard Swope, Franklin P. Adams, Heywood Broun–attract the continuing attention of writers and biographers. Mencken's accomplishments included success and recognition in editing, writing, criticism, and scholarship–any one of which merits success for any individual. Mencken excelled in all.

Unquestionably, the best way to know Mencken is to read him. Cooke's delightful *The Vintage Mencken* [1955], with a broad sampling of HLM's writings, provides a provocative introduction. A compact introduction to Mencken's life and works is available in Fitzpatrick's *H.L. Mencken* [1989]. Fecher's *Mencken: A Study of His Thought* [1978] provides a perceptive analysis of HLM's thought and his writing technique. "The Sage of Baltimore" and his role in that city is described in Dorsey's *On Mencken* [1980], with a delightful collection of essays.

Mencken's boyhood memoir, *Happy Days* [1940], encouraged into print by Harold Ross, captures his love affair with the

City of Baltimore; he lived almost his entire life in the same house on Hollins Street, excepting the five-year interval of his marriage. The early years formed his life-long views and prejudices. As a boy, Mencken read voraciously and played at being a newspaperman. He was awed by the ancient presses of the rural *Ellicott City Times* during vacation summers. Mencken declined college and toiled at the family cigar business until his father's death, then landed a job with the Baltimore *Morning Herald* in February 1899. His *Newspaper Days, 1899-1906* [1941] contains a romantic recounting of those years. Mencken, diligent and dutiful, kept his tobacco-selling job for some months, but regularly put in 10-and 12-hour days for the *Herald.* He had "been bustling with literary ardors" before 1895, he writes.

Mencken thought of himself as a newspaperman; it was the title he liked best. The third volume of his autobiographic trilogy, *Heathen Days, 1890-1936* [1943], deals with his newspaper exploits. The *Sunpapers* provided Mencken wide latitude, he was free to write a column (at first daily) and articles that afforded him outlet for assaults on American cultural icons. Bode's *The Young Mencken* [1973] includes generous examples of his formative work up to 1917, tackling a vast array of topics. His literary influences, Kipling and Shaw especially, were apparent. By 1908, he had produced three books: *Ventures into Verse; George Bernard Shaw: His Plays* and a translation, *The Philosophy of Friedrich Nietzsche.* Nietzsche's Superman, the elitist, became a leitmotif in much of Mencken's criticism.

Mencken was not so much an original thinker as an extraordinary prose craftsman who synthesized and embellished. His criticism of Shaw was the first ever undertaken. Clear parallels can be seen between Shaw and Mencken: both were journalists, both mounted frontal attacks on universal icons, both were elitists of the finest sort, and both rejected Democracy as a fraud.

Opportunity for a national pulpit came in 1908, when Mencken became book reviewer for the *Smart Set,* a magazine that became notable with Mencken's addition. Nolte's *Smart Set Criticism* [1968] provides a wide selection and little of this has been printed elsewhere. This period elicited some of HLM's best work. Nolte writes that Mencken is "credited quite rightly, with having been the leader of the forces for realism that triumphed

so completely in the nineteen-twenties." The *Smart Set* provided Mencken with an outlet for literary criticism of extraordinary
scope.

His Baltimore-based newspaper column enabled Mencken to
take on any individual or institution. This was a time of testing
and Rodgers' *The Impossible H. L. Mencken* [1991] contains
notable newspaper pieces that emerged in the twenties and thir-
ties. Mencken, however, was exploring themes that occupied his
attention for the next decade. He liked to "stir up the animals"
and did with considerable gusto. For example, commenting on
college suicides:

> What I'd like to see, if it could be arranged,
> would be a wave of suicides among college
> presidents. I'd be delighted to supply the pistols,
> knives, ropes, poisons and other necessary tools.
> A college student, leaping uninvited into the
> arms of God, pleases only himself. But a college
> president, doing the same thing, would give keen
> and permanent joy to great multitudes of persons.
> I drop the idea and pass on.

Mencken chose to remain in Baltimore and ventured to New
York to deliver his magazine copy and collect manuscripts, his
mode of operation through his entire career. Meanwhile, he
made useful connections with new and promising authors. His
books brought scant monetary success. A joint venture, *Men
Versus The Men* [1910] was a commercial failure as were two
books released in 1916: *A Book of Burlesques* and *A Little Book
in C Major.* Alfred A. Knopf published Mencken's first financial
success, *A Book of Prefaces* [1917]. The book was a literary success as well; this collection of newspaper and magazine pieces
was, writes Stenerson, nothing less than a "summons to rebel-
lion" against the Puritan influence that dominated American
culture. This was a crucial period in Mencken's life. In 1914, he
and George Jean Nathan gained joint editorship of the *Smart Set*
and turned it into a magnet for opinion and good writing. Any
mention of the war raging in Europe was excluded from its
pages. Mencken held a curious mental myopia in this regard.

An earlier ill-fated joint-venture publishing enterprise, *Europe After 8:15* [1914], failed utterly to consider the war's effect on society and was a dismal commercial failure. Meanwhile, Mencken fell into serious trouble with the *Sunpapers*. His violent anti-British, pro German stance (he defended the sinking of the *Lusitania* by noting, correctly, that it carried contraband) embarrassed the newspaper and his "Free Lance" column was canceled in October 1915. Mencken forever after saw this as an infringement on his right to free speech. Mencken found another outlet, the New York *Evening Mail,* and wrote a number of noteworthy pieces, including "The Sahara of the Bozart," and the "Neglected Anniversary." This later flummery was pure Mencken–his tongue-in-cheek version of the introduction of the bathtub to the White House. The hoax was swallowed by a number of scholars and citations of its authenticity continue. Later Mencken confirmed the fabrication as "all buncombe" and took delight in the academicians and newspapermen who had accepted the bogus story as truth without question.

Mencken produced two books in 1918, *Damn! A Book of Calumny* and *In Defense of Women.* Reviews were satisfactory, and to this day ardent feminists, missing Mencken's humor, take the *Defense* title literally. Sales and marketing were disappointing, but Mencken found his greatest publishing triumph in *The American Language* [1919]. This work grew from a series of articles stemming from his interest in language and was an instant critical success and Mencken's biggest money-maker; it sold more than a hundred thousand copies. Bode calls it a "classic" without reservation. Mencken scored another success in 1919 with a collection of *Smart Set* commentaries. *Prejudices: First Series* represents the best of his literary criticism, and was a success; so much so that five more volumes followed. Farrell collected a generous sampling in *Prejudices: A Selection* [1958].

By 1920, Mencken was back with the *Evening Sun* and in 1923, ties with *Smart Set* concluded, he embarked on a new magazine (backed by Alfred A. Knopf), the *American Mercury.* Mencken treated social issues with a personal, specific point of view. He encouraged writers to "depict and interpret the America that is in being; not the America that might be or ought to be" and solicited the "quacks" who "give good shows and offer salubrious instruction if only in the immemorial childishness of mankind." Editor Mencken promised these quacks "loving attention." The *Mercury,* a literary and financial success, established Mencken, editorialized the *New York Times,* "as the most powerful private citizen in America."

Mencken, intelligent and ambitious, had the energy and stamina ("I worked hard") to take on several roles simultaneously: a successful newspaperman, recognized as one of the best in the nation; a distinguished and talked-about author and critic whose books sold well; and editor of a leading magazine. Any of these attainments would have been rewarding for anyone. Mencken, vigorous and enterprising, surpassed himself in each of these endeavors in the 1920s.

After his return to the *Sunpapers* "Free Lance" was not resurrected. A Monday column ("articles" that might appear on a Saturday) produced the best newspaper writing in America over a span of eighteen years, earned HLM more fame, and assured the *Sun* a place in the top rank of American newspapers. The paper and Mencken played a major, national role in the 1925 Scopes trial that pitted Darwinian Evolution against Christian Fundamentalism and starred Williams Jennings Bryan, three-time Democratic presidential candidate and orator of "Cross of Gold" fame, against Clarence Darrow, the leading trial lawyer of the era. Manchester's biography of Mencken, *Disturber of the Peace,* benefits from Mencken's narrative version of the events. The trial, a stunt to gain publicity for an obscure Tennessee town, was orchestrated by Mencken, with the backing of his newspaper, into a national sensation. Mencken's role is described by Williams in *The Baltimore Sun: 1837-1987;* and *Thirty-five Years of Newspaper Work* adds Mencken's perspective. With hundreds of press and film media attending, Mencken became the central figure and defendant John Scopes was virtually ignored. The proceedings gave Mencken a stage on which to display the "idiocies" of Fundamentalism and his dispatches, Rodgers notes, included some of "the most brilliant in the history of journalism." The issue was neither religion nor free speech; the trial was a Mencken-managed event. Mencken filed copy unlikely to ever appear on page one in a general circulation metropolitan newspaper today. One excerpt:

The so-called religious organizations which
now lead the war against the teaching of
evolution are nothing more, at bottom, than
conspiracies of the inferior man against his
betters. They mirror very accurately his
congenital hatred of knowledge, his bitter enmity
to the man who knows more than he does, and
so gets more out of life...

Mencken produced excellent newspaper writing during the
Scopes trial, and *The Impossible Mr. Mencken* provides a baker's
dozen of his stories filed under deadline that should be required
reading in any reputable school of journalism. A series of weekly essays for the Chicago *Tribune* (1924-1928) dealt mostly with
literary matters–some of his best–with occasional forays into
social issues. Mencken's primary interest now centered on politics. His political commentaries–more than 700 in the *Evening
Sun*–are a vivid portrait of the people and events of that era.
Moos' *H.L. Mencken On Politics* [1956] provides a rich selection
for readers who, in these politically correct times, may be star-
tled at the tone in political reporting.

As editor of the *American Mercury,* Mencken was at zenith,
the most influential voice in American letters, described by
Nolte as "a literary dictator." A year after the Scopes trial,
Mencken again made national news with his vigorous defense of
First Amendment during the "Hatrack" incident. His blistering
defiance over censorship of the *Mercury* in state and federal
courts provided moral, if not legal, victory over Comstockery
and "morons" seeking to suppress the expression of ideas.
Manchester writes, "Mencken rose to the stature of a god."

Increasingly, however, much of his attention moved to politics. The *American Mercury* was the most influential magazine
of that era and Mencken's role as its founder and editor is recorded in several sources. Bode's *Mencken* provides an unbiased
account. Charles Angoff, an assistant on the magazine, reveals
an unflattering picture in *H.L. Mencken: Portrait from Memory*
[1956]. Knopf, owner of the *Mercury,* provides an intimate, less-
biased insider's view in *On Mencken.*

The declining fortunes of the *American Mercury* and the

erosion of Mencken's influence were related. The *Mercury*, with a targeted audience of 20,000 in 1924, soared to 80,500 by 1926, faltered after the stock market crash of 1929. The onset of the Great Depression, which Mencken then and afterward dismissed as a mere financial fluctuation, lost readers who had more pressing concerns to occupy their attention. Mencken refused to recognize the cataclysmic implications of America's economic collapse; he left the magazine in December 1933.

Mencken fell out of favor in the 1930s; iconoclasm was no longer fashionable, and his bellicosity became unpopular. He expressed scant concern for the ills brought on by the Depression and venomously opposed Franklin Roosevelt personally and the policies of the New Deal. His invective continued in the *Sunpapers*. Revisions for the *American Language* occupied him. The *Treatise on the Gods* [1930], his first book except for the *Prejudices* series since *Notes on Democracy* [1926], was a thoroughgoing dissection of religions that received good reviews and adequate sales, but failed to hold the attention of a public more concerned with economic troubles closer to home. His newspaper coverage of the nominating conventions of 1932, *Making a President,* sold poorly. His only major book was an historic overview of *The Sunpapers of Baltimore* [1937].

In 1942 he produced a long-time project, *A New Dictionary of Quotations.* Publication of his *Days* books in the 1940s and the satiric *Christmas Story* [1946] introduced Mencken to a new generation. Mencken, benign and eminently readable without the invective, was acceptable to readers emerging from the Depression. His *Chrestomathy* and his last work, *Minority Report* [1958], sustained Mencken's literary presence.

With the release of Mencken's sealed papers, a new series of published works, bolstered with intimate knowledge of HLM's private observations and written commentary, revealed aspects unknown in his public writings. Mencken, essentially a private person, nevertheless spent much time and money preparing his papers for housing in the Enoch Pratt and repositories elsewhere (to hedge against disasters, natural or otherwise) to be released at specified intervals for future examination.

Mencken's public version of his life and times can be found in the several *Days* books. Apparently, the fires had cooled and old combats were distant memories. His diary and memoranda, however, reveal a dark side that remembered every encounter. His private papers, written at the time of passion and partisanship, promised to set the record straight and settle old scores.

Publication of his *Diary*, covering 1930-1948, stimulated a storm of commentary when its contents implied (and its editor asserted) that Mencken was an anti-Semite, by today's standards a charge probably true. Mencken is no more than a reflection of his time and origin. Mencken was a man of contradictions, personal and private. Publicly, he attacked without malice and evident enthusiasm all groups and beliefs, and usually made a convincing case. He was a snob, an elitist and class-conscious and his writings reflect that view. Mencken held unconcealed contempt for democracy and viewed with undisguised scorn most of its inhabitants without regard to color, class, or creed. He invented and embellished established stereotypes. His views, amused and patronizing, infuriated large numbers of readers. Perhaps not surprisingly, his private views mirrored his public persona. He wrote from sincere, if narrow, beliefs.

The next harvest of the Mencken memoirs yielded his private comments as *Author and Editor.* Expectedly, the contents are a defense of his work and an assault on real and perceived enemies. Those seeking more evidence of Mencken's antipathy toward Jews will find it; others will find interesting HLM's withering scorn for his inferiors (practically everybody). He was petty, driven and ambitious, courted those who could assist him and dropped friends when they grew awkward or inconvenient. The portraits he draws are candid and without pity.

Mencken was outspoken and perhaps mean-spirited. He could embrace a questionable code of ethics that enabled him to be less than honest in his dealing with a no longer wanted publisher–a practice once admired as shrewd Yankee trading. To Mencken, it was a clever piece of chicanery. But times change and perhaps Mencken is not a likable person. Yardley presents Mencken unvarnished, without excuses.

Hobson's *Mencken: A Life* includes new material dealing with Mencken's personal life and many readers will conclude that in relations with women HLM was no gentleman. The

charge today would be that Mencken was a womanizer of the
worst sort. A number of female would-be contributors to his
magazine evidently found themselves in his bed and unpublished. Moreover, he attempted to suppress his letters to women
and theirs to him. In many respects, Mencken clearly felt that his
personal life was nobody's business and perhaps it is not. He
nevertheless attempted to alter the records, particularly regarding his relationships with women.

Hobson displays Mencken as a paradox: perhaps a private
bigot but a public figure who entertained blacks in his dining
room; an anti-Semite who warned against the eventual massacre
of Jews by the Nazis; an observer who dismissed Hitler as a
leader the good Germans would discard; a critic who plumbed
the philosophy of other writers but never expressed in depth his
own; and this most public of public men had a dark side, one of
lonely aloofness.

Fittingly, Mencken's latest work centers on his career as a
newspaperman, the role he relished. *Thirty-five Years of
Newspaper Work* deals with the years 1906-1941 at the
Sunpapers and holds special interest for journalism students,
teachers, newspaper people and historians. (For Mencken's public record on newspapering, Lippman's collection of HLM's observation of newspapers and the people involved, *A Gang of
Pecksniffs*, provides enlightening perspectives.) Mencken tells
something of this career in *Newspaper Days* and *Heathen Days*
but that was the public view, with no dirty laundry. *Thirty-five
Years* provides an intriguing account of Mencken's career and
continuing efforts to make the *Sun* a front-rank newspaper, the
best in America. The newspaper's failure to attain the stature
Mencken sought for the it, however, is part of the reason for his
chronicle of happenings major and minor in that frustrating pursuit and the dismal portrait of the people whom he felt impeded
his goal.

Mencken's private assessment of colleagues considered his
friends could be brutal, but illustrates that Mencken easily sepa-
rated professional evaluations from purely personal feelings. He
was a thoroughgoing professional and unforgiving toward others
who, in his estimation, were not. Few people measured up to his
personal work ethic. Personalities and office politics aside, con-

temporary readers will find this work rewarding for the commentary pertaining to making a newspaper first-rate. A number of the shortcomings continue to require attention in the industry. Mencken scoffed when newspapering was referred to as a "profession" and was unyielding in his contempt for schools of journalism and the results they produced.

His private papers reveal Mencken's frailties and foibles. Fecher's *Diary* introduced his deep prejudices; Yardley and Hobson demonstrate that Mencken was obsessed with his personal finances. He was almost pathological, noting and recording every penny of income and outgo with attentive and obsessive detail. Frugal but not ungenerous, he gave money freely to many friends and thoughtfully provided gifts. He could demonstrate uncommon generosity to some, but was often niggardly with those closest to him.

Mencken followed a strict code of honor, according to his lights, but his own accounting of petty deceits and prevaricating maneuvers raises questions. He would not lie, but often did not tell the truth. He was not above elliptical and evasive reasoning to justify dubious behavior. He sought out those who could aid him and coldly dropped bothersome friends of long standing. Often caring and considerate, he could be impervious to the effect his brusque manner had on those of lesser talent and blandly indifferent to adversities inflicted on others by fortune that they, unlike himself, failed to master.

But Mencken the man is not the yardstick for Mencken, the writer. Journalism classes could benefit from a study of Mencken's work. Students would enjoy his *Newspaper Days,* as history and an appreciation of the romance of what newspapering once was. Rodgers' collection of his newspaper stories in *The Impossible H.L. Mencken* is a treasure trove of good writing. *A Gang of Pecksniffs* contains acerbic commentary on ethics and newspapering; *Thirty-five Years of Newspaper Work* shows the inner workings of a modern newspaper and the efforts to improve. Mencken's pungent and outrageous commentary on life and letters and American politics cannot be dismissed because he was objectionable (especially when measured by the current standards of acceptable behavior). His humor, much underrated in his time and virtually overlooked today, deserves recognition for its originality and creativeness. Mencken ranks with Swift in his relentless satiric savaging of the body politic. No American writer except Mark Twain has managed to mount attacks cloaked with gentle humor and wound so deeply. But Twain was often irresolute; Mencken was relentless, unyielding, savage, and sardonic. Mencken was a writer of astonishing versatility and anyone venturing into his world of prose comes away enriched by a genius with the written word. Few were ever better.

REFERENCES

Betty Adler, *H.L.M.: The Mencken Bibliography* (Baltimore: The Johns Hopkins Press, 1961).

_____, *H.L.M.: The Mencken Bibliography: A Ten-Year Supplement* (Baltimore: Enoch Pratt Free Library, 1971).

Allison Busterbaum, *H.L. Mencken: A Research Guide* (New York: Garland Publishing Co., 1988).

Vincent Fitzpatrick, *H.L. Mencken* (New York: Ungar/ Continuum, 1989).

_____, *H.L. Mencken: The Mencken Bibliography: A Second Ten-Year Supplement, 1972-1981* (Baltimore: Enoch Pratt Free Library, 1986).

Fred Hobson, *H.L. Mencken: A Life* (New York Random House, 1994).

_____, *Serpent in Eden: H.L. Mencken and the South* (Chapel Hill: University of North Carolina Press, 1974).

Edward A. Martin, ed. *In Defense of Marion: The Love Letters of Marion Bloom and H.L. Mencken* (Athens: University of Georgia Press, 1996).

H.L. Mencken, *A Book of Prefaces* 5th ed. (Garden City, N.Y.: Doubleday, 1924).

_____, *A Gang of Pecksniffs: And Other Comments on Newspaper Publishers, Editors and Reporters,* Theo Lippman, ed. (New Rochelle, N.Y.: Arlington House, 1975).

_____, *A Mencken Chrestomathy* (New York: Vintage/ Random House, 1982).

_____, *A Second Chrestomathy,* Terry Teachout, ed. (New York: Knopf, 1995).

_____, *Christmas Story* (New York: Knopf, 1946).

_____, *H.L. Mencken's Smart Set Criticism,* 2d ed., William A. Nolte, ed. (Washington, D. C.: Gateway Edition, 1987).

_____, *Happy Days: 1880-1992* (New York: Knopf, 1940).

_____, *Heathen Days: 1890-1936* (New York: Knopf, 1943).

_____, *Mencken: A Study of His Thought,* Charles A. Fecher, ed. (New York: Knopf, 1978).

_____, *Mencken and Sara: A Life in Letters,* Marion Elizabeth Rodgers, ed. (New York: McGraw-Hill, 1987).

_____, *Minority Report: H.L. Mencken's Notebooks* (New York: Knopf, 1956/Johns Hopkins University Press, 1997).

_____, *My Life as Author and Editor,* Jonathan Yardley, ed. (New York: Knopf, 1993).

_____, *Newspaper Days: 1899-1906* (New York: Knopf, 1941).

_____, *On Mencken,* John Dorsey, ed. (New York: Knopf, 1980).

_____, *The Diary of H.L. Mencken,* Charles A. Fecher, ed. (New York: Knopf, 1989/Vintage, 1991).

_____, *The Vintage Mencken,* Alistair Cooke, ed. (New York: Vintage/Random House, 1955/1990).

_____, *The Impossible H.L. Mencken,* Marion Elizabeth Rodgers, ed. (New York: Anchor/Doubleday, 1991).

_____, *Thirty-five Years of Newspaper Work*, Fred Hobson, Vincent Fitzpatrick and Bradford Jacobs, eds. (Baltimore: Johns Hopkins University Press, 1994).

_____, *Ventures into Verse* (New York: Marshal, Beek and Goodman, 1903).

William Nolte, *H.L. Mencken: Literary Critic* (Middletown, Conn.: Wesleyan University Press, 1966).

Louis D. Rubin Jr., "An Honorable Profession: H.L. Mencken and the News," *Menckeniana* 131 (Fall 1944), 1-11.

Richard Schrader, *H.L. Mencken: A Descriptive Bibliography* (Pittsburgh: University of Pittsburgh Press, 1998).

Mark Sullivan, *Our Times: America at the Birth of the Twentieth Century,* abridged edition, Dan Rather, ed. (New York: Scribner/Simon & Schuster, 1996), 675-679.

Edmund Wilson, "The Aftermath of Mencken" [1969], *The Devils and Canon Barham* (New York: Farrar, Straus and Giroux, 1973).

Afterword

N O CLAIM IS PUT FORWARD here that every book that deals with the life and times of H.L. Mencken is discussed or identified in the foregoing discussions. Readers were forewarned. The collected essays here should be recognized for what they are: a modest overview and introduction, drawn from limited sources, that highlight specific aspects of Mencken's life and times. Surely, many books are mentioned here; many more are available for further reading and investigation. Critics may quibble that some of the issues are discussed in full elsewhere. If interest is piqued, however, go seek additional sources. If readers are persuaded to do that, a vast array of information awaits, the rewards bountiful, and the goal here met.

Mencken surely planned that future generations would have ample opportunity to explore deeper into his thoughts through his public papers. This is a writer's grasp for immortality. Mencken knew the fate of the Greek philosopher Chrysippus –the most-authoritative and most quoted of all the Stoics–whose works have vanished. And if perhaps Mencken doubted the Christian promise of everlasting life, he hedged his bet by doing what he could to assure that his earthly editorial activities provided evidence of his passage.

Mencken expended considerable time preparing his massive correspondence, manuscripts, and papers for archival reference primarily in Baltimore's Enoch Pratt Free Library, but also in a half-dozen other libraries and universities. Mencken was a prudent man and if one of his document mines were inaccessible because of disasters, natural or man-made, scholars would have opportunity to dig elsewhere. He spent considerable sums of money during his lifetime (and bequeathed a healthy inheritance) to see that these public papers were prepared in orderly fashion and received proper and reverent care for that specific purpose after his death.

A portion of his papers were deemed private–his diaries–and Mencken's grant of these papers to his executors stipulated specifically that these remain archival and private. Maryland legal authorities, however, ruled for publication and under the able editorship of Charles Fecher, a portion of these papers were published. Publication of his private thoughts led to charges that Mencken was a bigot, specifically anti-Semitic. These observations–concerning Jews, his friends and colleagues–were for his private diary; publicly, Mencken was outspoken and intolerant of everyone without exception. Mencken was a bigot who played no favorites.

Mencken was a figure who sought the limelight without ostentatious fanfare–he often dined at the Algonquin but avoided the boisterous "Round Table" celebrity circle favored by other writers. Like Mark Twain, Mencken did not wish to be conspicuous, but he did want to be noticed. Mencken was, in fact, a public figure who delighted in celebrity. He was an aloof individual, who sought to be apart from the crowd. He could, when moved, play a public role. For example, during the era when employers could be paternalistic, Mencken would perform with gusto as drum major, leading the Newsboy Band parade at the *Sunpapers'* annual picnic for hired hands at Baltimore's Bay Shore park. But that was family, hence permissible. Mencken was, at bottom, a private person who simply wanted his private diary, with his private thoughts, to be kept private. His relations with women, for example, were by his lights private and should remain so. He sought to suppress that correspondence and felt, properly, that this was a part of his private life that was nobody's business.

Now that those papers have been partially exposed, let some enterprising scholar look into them more fully. Large portions of the diaries remain unplumbed and may, in fact, yield additional facets that illuminate Mencken–his friends, his activities, and his interests. Perhaps more on his hypochondria may prove interesting to future readers. God knows, Mencken spent a portion of every day observing real and imagined ailments, which he dutifully recorded. Mencken was an inveterate visitor to sick-rooms and hospitals. (When his wife, Sara, lay dying from tuberculosis, however, visitations were painful and Mencken was absent a great deal; he simply could not bring himself to go.) More typically, acquaintances from all stations were apt to have Mencken appear, concerned and consoling, at their bedside to commiserate. Some read this as friendship; Mencken was merely being consultive. This was a typical Mencken character trait, like his inability to operate an automobile. He recorded all.

In fact, less than half of his public papers have been mined dealing with his years as an editor and more information may be found in the unexplored writings concerning his newspaper years. A full examination of his role as editor of the *Evening Sun's* editorial page remains to be chronicled. He was an unfair autocrat and a poor manager, but one hell of an editor.

Similarly, Mencken's full role as the leading participant for the Sunpapers during the Newspaper Guild negotiations has never been told and his papers should yield useful information of interest to newspaper managers and labor negotiators.

He was cast in even more unlikely roles. His letters disclose that Mencken was sounded out as a nominee for president of the University of Miami, in Coral Gables, a community carved from the outer Everglades near Miami, Florida. Mencken declined the academic post and dismissed the school as "a go-getting seminary founded by the realtors." (Relevant papers on the university side of the correspondence apparently disappeared in a fire.) A diligent search in the Mencken archives is apt to yield an interesting exchange. The mind boggles at the idea of Mencken at the helm of a university, especially one in the Deep South.

Mencken held a biased view toward higher education.; his formal education ended with graduation from high school. Academicians were scorned–"flatulent" was one of his milder epithets–and the feelings were mutual. Mencken's criticisms of academic literary efforts were dismissive and scored with deadly accuracy; academic rancor was his reward. Most of his scorn was directed at journalism schools–teachers and students.

Journalism schools, Mencken charged, were inept; with faculty comprised of failed newspapermen; attended by students too stupid to be admitted into credible academic programs; with snap courses and lax grading. Mencken was generally correct on all accounts and in many instances his charges remain valid.

Many of today's journalism faculty are as ignorant as the "third-raters" Mencken castigated more than fifty years ago. Many know Mencken only as a name, and have never heard of Eugene Field or Stanley Walker, for example, and remain blissfully unaware of the twenty years of excellent press criticism by Robert Benchley–all stellar journalists who never attended journalism school. No journalism school bears the name of one of the greatest newspapermen and editors of the twentieth century, and none is ever likely to; that would have been quite all right with Mencken.

Most of the papers that Mencken bequeathed to the Enoch Pratt remain unpublished and much remains for scholars to unearth that may prove interesting. For intrepid explorers much of what Mencken published remains unexamined. If Nolte skimmed much of the cream from Mencken's *Smart Set* criticisms, a great many of his columns remain unpublished in permanent form and that source should contain nourishing nuggets of information literary.

Similarly, opportunity beckons for some ambitious Ph.D. candidate to gather together all of Mencken's writings as Major Hatteras and his two dozen other pseudonyms. These observations served as the genesis or are clearly linked to other more substantive Mencken articles, essays, or books.

Hollins Street was a quiet oasis; no domestic pets except for a tortoise, genus *Terrapene,* nothing fancy–a simple box turtle. How many turtles over the years? No Menckenphile has yet to dig into the Hollins Street flowerbed to unearth the skeletal remains, but someone will eventually in all likelihood if the homestead stands. The future appears bleak.

Mencken's home is no monument. Municipal officials in Mencken's beloved Baltimore, as this is written, have for financial reasons, closed down Mencken's residence, long maintained as a museum (or shrine) to the city's most-renowned literary prize. The city that calls itself the "City that Reads" spent millions for an NFL team (the Ravens in homage apparently to Poe, who came to Baltimore to die) cannot afford the comparable pittance to maintain the home of a writer who spent more than 70 years in residence and crowned Baltimore with some distinction. Baltimore remains, as always, somewhat sluggish where opportunity is concerned. Consider. Asheville, North Carolina, now pays homage to Thomas Wolfe, despite his unhappy childhood in that obscure mountain hamlet in the recesses of the Blue Ridge, where residents were insulted to find themselves portrayed in his writings. Wolfe's home-hotel has been restored; an angel was added to the main thoroughfare for visitors to look to. Books are sold to those who can read. Wolfe himself never returned, but tourists flock in with money to spend.

Key West maintains a thriving cottage industry based on the fame of the some-time resident Ernest Hemingway, with books, t-shirts, cups and other memorabilia sold to raise expenses. Even Hemingway cats that inhabit the grounds constitute a brisk commodity to extract funds from tourists.

Ingenuity in Baltimore might disclose useful sources of revenue to reopen the Mencken home. For example, a Mencken turtle mart, properly managed and marketed with skill, could provide a source of revenue to support the Hollins Street property. This is a task that perhaps the Mencken Society might undertake with some reward. The Society remains a group that Mencken himself would have undoubtedly publicly dismissed with dark humor, but perhaps silently approved.

Mencken held himself aloof from seeking awards–no Pulitzer Prize adorns his memory. Indeed, he dismissed such baubles–he convinced Sinclair Lewis to reject a Pulitzer and blamed Lewis's second wife, Dorothy Thompson, for unseemly zeal when Lewis accepted the Nobel prize for Literature. His long-time employer, the *Sunpapers,* grants an annual Mencken prize to the modern journalist who most exemplifies Mencken's iconoclastic tradition. With some notable exceptions, however, few recipients are apt to be remembered for noteworthy contributions, either to journalism or to writing. But the award serves to keep his memory alive, and Henry Mencken would have liked that.

Mencken could not exist today. The times simply would not permit it. No media source would allow Mencken to deliver so freely–and gleefully–vituperative and accurate observations on the body politic or the imbecilities of the populace. No major newspaper would allow any writer to exercise the kind of opinion that Mencken put forth regularly concerning political leaders, events, and commentary on happenings of his day. Political correctness–the contemporary censor of free speech and thought, as invidious as the Salem witch hunts or McCarthyism–prohibits the kind of expression that Mencken exercised so freely. His invective and name-calling would be neither condoned nor tolerated. Most of Mencken's really outrageous commentary was confined to his magazines and his books. Books then, and now, are read by relatively few. Modern mass media would never foster a talent like Mencken.

No modern communication enterprise with an eye on the bottom line would allow any hired hand to play such a prominent role. Consider that one of the greatest journalists of unquestioned integrity was brought to heel; corporate CBS could not tolerate an Edward R. Murrow and reined in this giant of the television era. Today CBS–and every other network–is part of a vast conglomerate that is greater than the sum of the talent it hires. As Mencken feared, the First Amendment has eroded. Mencken would not survive today, not on a newspaper or mass magazine or television. The best that a modern Mencken could aspire to is that an amiable publisher might print his books to be read by an erudite audience of eccentric cranks.

Mencken would praise where he saw fit to praise, which was not very often. Mostly, he viewed with disdain or disfavor the behavior of fellow infesters of the planet and reported it with zestful humor and cutting observation, not exempting himself from his sallies. For what his fellow creatures thought of him–and hardly anyone was indifferent–Mencken dismissed them succinctly: "I don't give a damn what any American thinks of me."

Appendix

Books by H. L. Mencken

BOOKS LISTED are either solely by Mencken or co-written by him; omitted are collections of letters and correspondence and minor works HLM edited (* denotes books in print); original publishers are noted with year of publication and reprints have the publications and year.

1903 *Ventures Into Verse* (Marshall, Beck & Gordon)

1905 George Bernard Shaw: His Plays (Luce/Haskell, 1989)*

1908 *The Philosophy of Friedrich Nietzsche*
(Luce/Transaction, 1993)*

1910 *Men Versus The Man: A Correspondence Between Rives La Monte, Socialist and H.L. Mencken, Individualist,* with Rives La Monte (Holt)

1914 *Europe After 8:15,* with George Jean Nathan and Williard Huntington Wright (Lane)

1916 *A Book of Burlesques* (Lane/Scholarly, 1992)*

1916 *A Little Book in C Major* (Lane)

1917 *A Book of Prefaces* (Knopf/Reprint Services, 1992)*

1918 *Damn! A Book of Calumny* (Goodman)

1918 *In Defense of Women* (Goodman/Knopf, 1992/Time-Life Books, 1982)

1919 *The American Language: A Preliminary Inquiry Into the Development of English in the United States* (Knopf/Abridged Edition, Raven I. MacDavid, ed., 1963)*

1919 *Prejudices: First Series* (Knopf)

1920 *The American Credo: A Contribution Toward the Interpretation of the National Mind,* with George Jean Nathan (Knopf)

1920 *Prejudices: Second Series* (Knopf)

1922 *Prejudices: Third Series* (Knopf)

1924 *Prejudices: Fourth Series* (Knopf)

1925 *Americana: 1925,* ed. H.L. Mencken (Knopf)

1926 *Americana: 1926,* ed. H.L. Mencken (Knopf)

1926 *Notes on Democracy* (Knopf)

1926 *Prejudices: Fifth Series* (Knopf)

1927 *Prejudices: Sixth Series* (Knopf)

1927 *Selected Prejudices* (Knopf)

1928 *Menckeniana: A Schimpflexikon,* ed. H.L. Mencken (Knopf)

1930 *Treatise on the Gods* (Knopf/Johns Hopkins, 1996)*

1932 *Making a President: A Footnote to the Saga of Democracy* (Knopf)

1934 *Treatise on Right and Wrong* (Knopf)

1937 *The Sunpapers of Baltimore: 1837-1937,* with Gerald W. Johnson, Frank R. Kent and Hamilton Owens (Knopf)

1940 *Happy Days, 1880-1892* (Knopf/Johns Hopkins, 1996)*

1941 *Newspaper Days, 1899-1906* (Knopf/Johns Hopkins, 1996)*

1942 *A New Dictionary of Quotations on Historic Principles from Ancient and Modern Sources,* ed. H.L. Mencken (Knopf)*

1943 *Heathen Days, 1890-1936* (Knopf/Johns Hopkins, 1996)*

1945 *Supplement I, The American Language* (Knopf)*

1946 *Christmas Story* (Knopf)

1947 *The Days of H.L. Mencken: Happy Days,*
    Newspaper Days, Heathen Days (Knopf/Dorset,
    1990)*

1948 *Supplement II, The American Language* (Knopf)*

1949 *A Mencken Chrestomathy* (Knopf/Vintage)*

1955 *The Vintage Mencken,* ed. Alistair Cooke, (Knopf)*

1956 *Mencken on Politics: A Carnival of Buncombe,*
    ed. Malcolm Moos, (Vintage/Johns Hopkins, 1996)*

1956 *Minority Report: H.L. Mencken's Notebooks*
    (Knopf/Johns Hopkins, 1997)*

1958 *A Bathtub Hoax and Other Blasts and Bravos*
    from the Chicago Tribune, ed. Robert McHugh
    (Knopf)

1958 *Prejudices: A Selection,* ed. James T. Farrell
    (Vintage/Johns Hopkins, 1996)*

1959 *H. L. Mencken's Days: Happy Days, Newspaper*
    Days, Heathen Days (Dorset)*

1961 *H. L. Mencken on Music,* ed. Louis Cheslock
    (Knopf/Reprint Service, 1990)*

1963 *The American Language* (abridged), Supplements
    I and II, ed. Raven I. McDavid Jr. (Knopf)*

1965 *The American Scene: A Reader,* ed. Huntington Cairns
    (Knopf/Vintage, 1982)*

1968 *H. L. Mencken's Smart Set Criticism,* ed. William H.
    Nolte(Cornell University Press/Gateway, 1987)*

1973 *On Being an American and other Essays,*
    ed. Shigehisa Narita (Kenkyusha)

1973 *The Young Mencken: The Best of His Work,*
    ed. Carl Bode (Dial)

1975 *A Gang of Pecksniffs and Other Comments on*
    Newspaper Publishers, Editors and Writers,
    ed. Theo Lippman (Arlington House)

1976 *Mencken's Last Campaign: H. L. Mencken on the 1948 Election* ed. Joseph C. Goulden (New Republic Books)

1980 *A Choice of Days*, ed. Edward C. Galligan (Knopf)*

1988 *The Editor, the Bluenose and the Prostitute*, ed. Carl Bode (Roberts Rinehart)*

1989 *The Diary of H. L. Mencken*, ed. Charles A. Fecher (Knopf/Vintage, 1991)*

1991 *The Impossible H. L. Mencken:A Selection of His Best Newspaper Stories*, ed. Marion Elizabeth Rodgers (McGraw-Hill/Anchor, 1991)*

1993 *My Life as Author and Editor*, ed. Jonathan Yardley (Knopf/Vintage, 1995)*

1994 *Thirty-five Years of Newspaper Work: A Memoir by H. L. Mencken*, ed. Fred Hobson, Vincent Fitzpatrick and Bradford Jacobs (Johns Hopkins)*

1995 *A Second Mencken Chrestomathy*, ed.Terry Teachout (Knopf/Vintage, 1995)*

Index